CAUGHT IN CROSSFIRE

Modern Irish Society
(Appletree Press)

Irish Studies
(Syracuse University Press)

CAUGHT IN CROSSFIRE

Children and the Northern Ireland Conflict

Ed Cairns

APPLETREE PRESS
SYRACUSE
UNIVERSITY PRESS

First published and printed by
The Appletree Press Ltd
7 James Street South
Belfast BT2 8DL
1987

British Library Cataloguing
in Publication Data
Cairns, Ed
Caught in Crossfire: Children and the
Northern Ireland Conflict.
1. Children—Northern Ireland
I. Title
305.2'3'09416   HQ792.G7

ISBN 0-86281-186-4

Published in the United States by
Syracuse University Press
Syracuse
New York 13244-5160

ISBN 0-8156-2421-2

9 8 7 6 5 4 3 2 1

Manufactured in Ireland

With love to
Ida, Tara, Clare and Ryan

So, since this ruptured country is my home,
It long has been my luck to be
Caught in the cross-fire of their false campaign.

John Hewitt
'The Dilemma', 1969

Contents

Preface

This is a book that I have been thinking about writing for some time. Several things stopped me from doing it sooner. Apart from all the usual reasons one has for not doing such things perhaps what most held me up was my conscience. Was it right to gain, in any way, from others' misfortunes – especially when those others were young children? Eventually I decided that there was just the possibility that children in Northern Ireland, and in other parts of the world where community conflict rages, had also something to gain from such a book.

Perhaps the most important way this could happen is simply by making sure that people in other parts of the world become familiar with what is known about children in Northern Ireland, what they have suffered, how they have borne this suffering and why they have had to suffer. The book therefore begins by considering the consequences, both physical and psychological, for children of living in Northern Ireland. It then moves on to look at the causes of the conflict and ends by trying to suggest how the future may look to the next generation.

To do all this I have tried to summarise, in non-technical language if possible, the large amount of research material that has been accumulated to date in this area. I happen to believe that academic knowledge is too important to be left to the academics. This is not therefore a book only for psychologists, indeed it is not, I hope, a book only for academics but one which, in the spirit of George Miller, 'gives psychology away'. For this reason also, I have tried to make this a short book in the hope that it will be affordable to even the most impoverished student.

Of course this knowledge which I am trying to give away is only available because of the dedicated and painstaking efforts of my colleagues in psychology and the other social sciences who have risked a great deal, as Chapter 1 points out, in their attempts to discover 'the truth' about life in Northern Ireland for the young people who live there. My own contribution to this effort has been to bring together in one volume the fruits of their labour. I therefore wish to take this opportunity to publicly recognise the dedication of these colleagues both here in Northern Ireland and in other countries throughout the world and to thank them on behalf of the children of Northern Ireland.

Particularly I would like to take this opportunity to thank all those who have encouraged me both to write this book and to continue to work in this area. Where the book is concerned John Darby, the Director of the Centre for the Study of Conflict at the University of Ulster was the principal stimulus and support. Seamus Dunn and Jerry Harbison along with John Darby were kind enough to read parts of the manuscript while Pat Shortt was patient enough to decipher my handwriting and type and retype the many drafts that ensued.

However, even before I reached that stage I was supported and encouraged by many colleagues and students too numerous to mention who shared with me the pain and pleasure of working in this area. Of these I would like to single out Halla Beloff and Ken Heskin who early on in my career tried at least to make sure that I started out on the right path as well as Bill Mercer and Ronnie Wilson with whom much of my own research work has been undertaken.

Finally I wish to take this opportunity to record my love and gratitude to my wife and children to whom this book is dedicated.

1

The Troubles

Northern Ireland is a small dot on the world map – some 5,452 square miles in all. Its population is equally small although rather more of them are children and young people than in most western countries (over one third) and the birth rate continues to be somewhat higher than in most other European countries.

Nevertheless only about half a million young people (under seventeen years) live in Northern Ireland. Why therefore write a whole book about a small number of children living in the northern half of a small off-shore European island? The answer is of course that these children have lived through the longest period of concentrated civil disturbances to have hit the western world in modern times. And the world is naturally curious as to how the children of Ulster have coped. Has growing up against a backdrop of bombs, explosions, assassinations and riots produced a totally amoral generation of potential psychopaths, a shell-shocked generation of neurotics or has it had any effect at all? And what of the hatred that apparently fuels violence in Northern Ireland. Has that been passed on to the next generation or has the horror of the past, the continuous violence, led to war weariness and made the young people of Northern Ireland turn away from violence to seek a more peaceful solution to their age-old quarrel?

These are the sort of questions this book will attempt to answer and to answer not on the basis of opinion but if at all possible on the basis of empirical facts. Before beginning to sort through the evidence that is available in an attempt to learn 'the truth' about the children of Ulster it is worth pausing to consider the background against which this information has been obtained, the strengths and the limitations of the existing information and in doing so to sketch in some pertinent facts about Northern Irish society.

The Role of the Media

Before 1969 the children of Northern Ireland were of little interest to the world in general or indeed even to local social scientists. Then the media, especially television, horrified viewers all over the world by showing children, including pre-schoolers, engaging the might of the British army nightly on the streets of Belfast and Derry. Within a short space of time Ulster's children had become a favourite topic for headline writers and photographs of children in Northern Ireland, stones in hand, had begun to appear regularly on the covers of weekly magazines. Some 2,000 plus deaths and almost twenty years later the media still take an, albeit somewhat less intense, interest in the children of Northern Ireland but in the interim their interest has sparked a burgeoning social science literature in this area. It would be untrue therefore to say that the violence has only made life worse for young people in Northern Ireland without bringing any benefits at all in its wake. The one benefit young people have derived from the conflict is that at the very least it has served to focus attention on them and on issues long neglected in the past. The important point here is that while, to the average person elsewhere, Northern Ireland and its problems may have appeared to suddenly pop out of nowhere on to their television screens, in reality the conflict in Northern Ireland has a much longer history dating back, some would argue, for at least 300 years (*see* Darby, 1983). During this period there has not been continuous violence although it would be true to say there has been continuous conflict. Nevertheless in this century alone and particularly since Ireland was partitioned in the 1920s leading to the creation of Northern Ireland (or Ulster as it is sometimes referred to) as a part of the United Kingdom, along with England, Scotland and Wales and as a separate entity from the remainder of Ireland (which constitutes the Republic of Ireland) violence has broken the surface at least four times, in the 1920s, the 1930s, the 1950s and most recently beginning in 1969-70.

The question then is why, if political conflict and indeed violence have been problems that have been around in Northern Ireland for so long, did social scientists only become interested in Ulster's children relatively recently? Why did it take the glare of the world's media spotlight before even local social scientists began to investigate issues that they must surely have been aware of? Whatever the reason, their failure to do so presents a major problem to anyone wishing to examine the impact of the recent civil disturbances (or 'the troubles' as they are known locally) on the children of Northern Ireland. The problem is that very little information exists about children before the current disturbances began and therefore making before and after comparisons becomes exceedingly difficult.

It is important not to dismiss the lack of pre-1969 interest by social scientists in young people in Northern Ireland as a mere nuisance. Rather it can be argued that this is in itself an important piece of information about the kind of society Northern Ireland was and perhaps still is. Various explanations have been put forward as to why Northern Ireland had to totter to the brink of civil war and become the focus of the world's media before the interest of local social scientists was awakened to the questions of violence and sectarianism which had undoubtedly existed before 1969. One simple explanation (or is it an excuse?) is that while violence has a long, and one could even say respected, tradition in Ireland, the social sciences have not. Another popular hypothesis is that there was what amounts to a conspiracy of silence on the part of social scientists. But again this begs the question why? One possibility is that this silence was the result of domination by the 'establishment'. Certainly the establishment in the past does not appear to have encouraged research related to Northern Ireland's social problems and while this has now undergone a radical change even today one can at times still detect something of the ostrich syndrome in establishment circles.

But even this argument is not entirely convincing. Why did local social scientists allow themselves to be part of the conspiracy of silence if indeed such a conspiracy existed? To answer this question one has to understand that over the years the people of Northern Ireland have attempted to arrive at a working solution to deal with, at an interpersonal level, their deeply held differences focussing largely on whether Northern Ireland should continue to be part of the United Kingdom (the Protestant view) or part of a United Ireland (the Catholic view). And one solution arrived at seems to have been a general agreement not to mention these differences in 'mixed' (i.e. Catholic and Protestant) company except perhaps on formal political occasions. The result has been that politics/religion (they are difficult to disentangle in Ulster) has been a taboo subject similar perhaps to sex in other societies – that is not to be mentioned in polite circles unless one is very sure that one is in the company of close friends. Perhaps this taboo has provided something of a safety valve even today preventing political differences spilling over into personal relationships. Undoubtedly therefore in the past social scientists may have felt that to attempt to mention this taboo topic even in a research context would not only be breaking a strongly held social convention but would also possibly upset the barely maintained political equilibrium which balanced Northern Irish formal politics against sectarian violence. No doubt some well-meaning folk elsewhere felt that Kinsey's early research on sexual behaviour would, by bringing such things into the open, unleash a wave of debauchery on civilised society. Similarly responsible people in Northern Ireland felt that to discuss politics and religion openly could only lead to one thing – violent conflict. In fact it is likely that nothing could be further from the truth, a point which will be returned to in the final chapter.

Ethical Problems

If one accepts this explanation for the lack of research before the current troubles began, what also then has to be explained is why, once the violence was in full spate and Northern Ireland's politics were being openly discussed by the world's press, local social scientists were still rather slow to get research under way. One reason is that, paradoxically, when the violence was at its height the earlier taboo still held. Thus researchers in Northern Ireland still had to face the criticism that by asking questions about views on politics or religion they were engaging in acts which were 'destructive of community relations.' And this attitude can still persist today as Trew and McWhirter (1982) report. An investigation of theirs in 1981 resulted in a local politician calling for a public enquiry and claim and counter-claim by politicians and investigators in the local press as to the merits or otherwise of their research.

Also new hurdles now appeared which researchers in Northern Ireland had to overcome though still related to the general topic of the ethics of research in a divided society. For example, in any social science research the question of protecting the privacy of individual informants is of paramount importance. However, in the volatile situation in Northern Ireland which developed during the 1970s, as Beloff (1980) noted, encroachment on privacy took on a special meaning. This special meaning relates to the fact that disclosure of a source by a social science researcher in Northern Ireland may not simply lead to embarrassment for the individual concerned but could actually involve physical danger, and ultimately the threat of death. This of course has meant that, depending on the topic, persuading individuals to participate in social science research can be a major problem. The result has been that many questionnaires and interviews have been conducted under the guise of anonymity, which in turn, it could be argued, may detrimentally affect the quality of responses and certainly rules out the possibility of any type of follow-up study. And being involved in social science research in Northern Ireland can mean stress for the investigator as well as the respondents as some investigators have reported (Fields, 1973; Russell, 1974; Burton, 1979). Part of the problem here is that in a bi-confessional society such as Northern Ireland there are two versions of everything – schools, voluntary organisations, sports associations and, inevitably, two versions of 'the truth'. Therefore, one of the problems faced by the social science researcher is that of being accused of taking sides. Of course, on some occasions this may have happened and some research, one suspects, has been undertaken not to discover 'the truth' but rather 'to actively proselytise on behalf of particular versions of reality' (Taylor and Nelson, 1977). It should be said however that such studies have been the exception rather than the rule. Yet the very possibility that social scientists may not be immune to taking sides or simply that a neutral view of 'the truth' will not be acceptable to one or even both sides has hampered research. This is because, one suspects, local social scientists have steered clear of topics on which there already exist two very obvious versions of reality and secondly, because research co-operation has not been easy to obtain as local institutions in particular may have suspected that local researchers may not always be unbiased. Indeed, for this reason it has been claimed that researchers from other countries have been more readily accepted by both sides in Northern Ireland and have thus been able to undertake research closed to local social scientists (Fields, 1973).

If researchers in Northern Ireland have been afraid that their findings will not be accepted by people in Northern Ireland, they have also feared that their findings will be too readily accepted, particularly by the media, who are always suspected of being ready to sensationalise or at least oversimplify Northern Irish issues. Also policy-makers, struggling in the vacuum created by the lack of empirical knowledge on which to base their decisions, are suspect in this regard. Social scientists carry this sort of responsibility in any society but in Northern Ireland it is perhaps more keenly felt. Fields, an American researcher, has put it most eloquently, describing how she felt as she began to face the problem of writing her book on Northern Ireland:

I'm overwhelmed with this responsibility and very afraid now – more afraid than I was at any time in Belfast : [then] I carried responsibility only for myself. This time, I am faced with carrying responsibility for making explicit the many and amorphous conditions of human existence in a beleagured and bleeding island. (Fields, 1973, 26)

These ethical problems of course apply to all research conducted in Northern Ireland but apply with particular force to that research which has young people as its primary focus. Children are particularly vulnerable in all sorts of ways as research participants. For example, they are much less likely to exercise or indeed even recognise their right to refuse to participate in research. Russell (1973) gives a good example of the problems of working with children in Northern Ireland; he found that younger children would often volunteer *more* information than was really required and that just occasionally their stories might have a factual basis. This became especially worrying when the stories were about older members of the family possessing weapons or being in illegal organisations. For this reason he notes one study was abandoned through fear of uncovering too much information for his own good!

Another ethical issue that has exercised researchers in Northern Ireland involved with children has been that of sensitising children to various issues. As Cairns (1980) has noted the problem is that the very act of interrogating children on a particular topic may mean that the researcher is in fact unintentionally providing information about topics of which the children may have been up to then entirely innocent. To overcome this problem researchers working with children have often resorted to indirect methods for interrogating children, often in very imaginative ways. Unfortunately this in turn also means that a question mark inevitably hangs over the interpretation of data obtained in this way.

These kinds of ethical issues noted above undoubtedly retarded social science research in Northern Ireland, particularly research with children and particularly before the current spate of 'the troubles' brought the whole thing out in the open. However, one further factor remains which may help to explain why local researchers were so slow off the mark in this area and even today could be accused of dragging their feet. This is the fact that, as Heskin (1980a) put it, local social scientists may have been 'intimidated by the complexity of the situation viewed from a vantage point or perhaps a disadvantage point of local knowledge.'

Poverty in Northern Ireland

To those readers who only know about Northern Ireland through the images they have seen on their television screen it may come as something of a surprise to suggest that there could be anything complex about what is happening there. Northern Ireland's media image has been that of a simple society with a simple two-sided problem, that of a medieval religious war, perhaps, or a colonial struggle. However, anyone who knows the place at first hand, especially someone who has lived there all their life, realises that this media image is, inevitably, a gross oversimplification. What the one-minute television reports tend to ignore is the fact that Northern Ireland has problems other than those of sectarian violence and indeed that even the violence is itself a complex ever-changing phenomenon.

Perhaps the single most important fact ignored by the media about Northern Ireland is that it has the unenviable reputation of being the least affluent region of the United Kingdom and is offically recognised as one of the least prosperous areas within the European Economic Community (Simpson, 1983). Further, there is evidence that this relative poverty is nothing new to this part of the world and is not, for example, something which has been caused by the recent civil disturbances. Rather Simpson (1983) suggests that poverty in Northern Ireland predates the Second World War and indeed probably can be traced back further than the creation of Northern Ireland as a separate entity in the 1920s.

Local social scientists are of course only too well aware of this state of affairs and of the fact that poverty can have as great an impact on peoples' lives as can violence, if not greater. In particular social scientists interested in children in Northern Ireland are very conscious of the fact that violence is not the only form of deprivation that Northern Ireland's children may have been exposed to. Indeed, for some children in Northern Ireland poverty makes its impact from the very first days of life in that the infant mortality rate in Northern Ireland has, for over twenty years, been considerably higher than in other areas. Fortunately improvements have been made during this period but the rate in 1981 was still higher than in England and Wales (Compton and Coward, 1983). Those children lucky enough to survive beyond infancy still face other potential hazards – growing up in large families in overcrowded homes, homes which do not always possess all of the basic amenities and in homes where unemployment is a relatively common fact of life for about 25 per cent of the adult population. Nor does this poverty affect only a small minority of children in Northern Ireland. Evason (1976) has estimated that in 1975 over 30 per cent of all children in Northern Ireland lived in what could officially be described as a 'low income family.' This position is not improving as Bush and Marshall (1983) report a similar figure for 1979 (34 per cent). Further, they suggest that, given the rise in unemployment levels since 1979, this may be an underestimate.

Perhaps the worst aspect, or at least one might imagine the most demoralising aspect, of Northern Ireland's poverty is that for the generation of children growing up in the 1970s and 1980s the prospects of ever escaping the cycle of deprivation are slim.

Children only have to look around their own family circle in certain areas of Northern Ireland to see that not only are their fathers and uncles not employed now but that they have been unemployed for very long periods of time, perhaps for all their 'working' lives. And for the next generation the prospects are no better. In 1982 of those children leaving school and seeking employment 75 per cent became unemployed.

Violence in Northern Ireland

Of course, social deprivation in Northern Ireland gets little publicity abroad for two very good reasons. First the poverty is relative, relative that is to the more affluent parts of the western world. And second, poverty is by no means unique to Northern Ireland. All this is of little comfort to Northern Ireland but it does at least help to explain why the media and social scientists alike tend to concentrate on the violence alone. Because what makes Northern Ireland unique is undoubtedly the fact that it has endured internally generated violence for such a sustained period. Yet on the face of it nine or ten deaths a month for fifteen years may not seem particularly startling. However, when one considers the thousands more who have been injured – many of them maimed for life in various horrible ways – and when these figures are considered in relation to the size of Northern Ireland's population then a new perspective emerges. Put at its most dramatic if the same violence had occurred on the same scale in the USA then more than a quarter of a million people would be dead by now. The impact these deaths have had on the population of Northern Ireland has therefore been marked, indeed Rose (1976) has suggested that by 1975 nearly one family in every six must have had a relative killed or injured in the troubles.

But even these statistics do not do justice to the complexity of Northern Ireland's violence. Again the media picture of violence in Northern Ireland has been very much one-dimensional. Local social scientists however have been only too well aware of the intricacies that lie behind the bald statistics. In particular they have been conscious of the fact that the very use of the phrase 'the violence' glosses over both spatial and temporal dimensions of which the outsider is often not aware. In other words, the violence over the last fifteen years has not been an all-embracing steady stream of violent incidents but rather has varied greatly both from time to time and from place to place.

Northern Ireland consists largely of a series of fairly tightly knit communities. Even Belfast, its largest city and capital (population half a million) where about one third of the population of Northern Ireland lives has been described as a collection of villages rather than a city. Also, compared to the rest of the United Kingdom, Northern Ireland has a much more rural population, 45 per cent as opposed to 30 per cent. Finally, residential segregation on a religious basis is not uncommon.

Given this demographic background it is perhaps not surprising to learn that all areas of Northern Ireland have not experienced the current spate of violence in a uniform way. This is best illustrated by the fact that Poole (1983) was able to list twenty-seven towns in Northern Ireland, each with a population greater than 5,000, where deaths per thousand due to political violence in the period 1969-81 ranged from a maximum of 1.91 to a minimum of zero. Further, seven of these towns had experienced one or more deaths per thousand in this period while four had experienced no fatalities at all. Explanations for these variations in the level of political violence need not concern us unduly here although this has been the subject of much careful research (Mitchell, 1979; Murray, 1982; Poole, 1983; Schellenberg, 1977). Poole (1983) concludes that the ethnic composition of an area is an important factor, particularly the size of the local Catholic population relative to the local Protestant population with a relatively larger Catholic population predictive of greater levels of violence. Whatever the explanation, the important implication, for those who wish to study the impact of the troubles on the children of Ulster, is that ideally they should make clear which children from which part of Ulster they are referring to. Indeed, simply selecting children from one particular town may not be a guarantee of equal exposure because even within towns, especially the larger towns such as Belfast and Derry, areas may exist side by side where one has been subjected to extreme violence while the other is an apparent haven of peace and security.

This is in fact a feature of Northern Irish life which is relatively obvious to the most naive visitor. Often such a person is surprised that within a short distance of each other can be found areas which bristle with the impedimenta of internal security operations – fortified police stations, armed soldiers wearing bullet-proof vests on street patrol, road blocks, armoured personnel carriers in the streets – and those in which the only sign of security may be a policeman on a pedal cycle.

However, while the spatial aspect of Northern Ireland's violence is thus open to inspection, a more subtle feature is the temporal dimension. In other words, the fact that the intensity of violence varies not only from place to place at any one time but also in intensity from time to time. Statistics show that the rise and fall of violence in Northern Ireland, as measured for example by the numbers of deaths per year, has been quite marked. To those outside Northern Ireland it may appear that the violence drones endlessly on from year to year, a constant in the equation that makes up the life of the province. This is in fact far from the truth and locals readily distinguish good years from bad.

For example, 1972 was a very bad year, with almost 500 deaths, the worst year in fact since the troubles began in 1969. On the other hand 1984 was, by comparison, a good year, with only 64 deaths. In fact the violence to date, as charted by the number of deaths per year, can be seen to have gone through three distinct phases. The violence, beginning in 1969, showed a slow rise over the first three years to 1971 followed by a quadrupling to the enormity of 468 deaths in 1972. After this, for the next four years, deaths per year fell, but were still high with an average of about 250 per year. Since then, for at least the last six years, Northern Ireland has experienced what an English politican once crassly described as 'an acceptable level of violence', averaging about 95 deaths per year.

The practical implications of these statistics for social scientists interested in studying the effects of the troubles on children in Northern Ireland and indeed for the reader of this book interested in attempting to understand that research, is that children questioned in different years may well have experienced differing levels of exposure to violence. This is neatly illustrated in a study by Cairns, Hunter and Herring (1980). In this study young children (five to six years) were asked to make up stories about drawings which depicted such things as a derelict house or a train crash. What interested the investigators was the number of times the children suggested bombs or explosions as an explanation for what they saw in the pictures presented to them. Two studies were carried out along these lines and a puzzling result was that in the first study some 90 per cent of the children from Northern Ireland mentioned bombs or explosions compared to only 45 per cent in the second study. At first the investigators thought perhaps some change in procedure could account for the difference, for example the fact that the first lot of children were interviewed by a woman, the second lot by a man. The final explanation however was that the data in the first study were gathered at the end of 1976 when 766 explosions occurred in Northern Ireland compared to 1977 when the data for the second study were obtained and in which year there were 'only' 295 explosions.

Finally, not only has the violence varied in terms of where it has happened and when it has happened but also how it has happened. That is to the spatial and temporal dimensions one must add a qualitative dimension. The earliest violence consisted almost exclusively of street rioting – hence the image of the 'typical' Ulster child, stone in hand, still prevalent around the world. This period of street violence on a large scale did not actually last very long – only a year or two – and while street rioting is not unknown today, and indeed may be staging something of a comeback, it now tends to occur only on a relatively small local scale. Today the violence is dominated not by confrontation between large groups of people over long periods of time but rather by armed action often involving only one or two people and possibly lasting only seconds. This is because after 1971 the violence has been largely the preserve of the paramilitary organisations and the security forces. Yet even in this struggle there have been qualitative changes over time particularly in the type of weapon favoured by the paramilitaries.

These alterations in tactics and weaponry have been mainly in response to counter measures employed by the other side – that is the security forces – and have as a result led to an increasing sophistication in the methods used to kill and maim. Over the years therefore the people of Northern Ireland have witnessed technological advances which have led from the parcel bomb (left on the doorstep) to car bomb to miniaturised incendiary bomb to bombs remotely controlled either mechanically or by radio. Similarly, the paramilitaries' other weapons have grown from hand guns and rifles through high-powered machine guns to Russian made rocket launchers.

The targets of violence have also changed from time to time, although commercial and government property have continued to be popular over the years as have members of the security forces both on and off duty. Where people have been concerned, the changes have been rung frequently to include prison officers, members of the judiciary and plainly random sectarian killings. White (1983) writing on this topic suggests that these changes have been a deliberate tactic in order to maintain a feeling of insecurity in all sectors of the population. Nor have all the deaths been due to paramilitary violence because the response to this has often been increased activity on the part of the security forces. This in turn has perhaps inevitably led to more deaths and not always of proven terrorists. As in any 'war' the innocent have suffered along with the guilty.

As far as social science investigations are concerned all this becomes a further complicating factor because people, and particularly children, undoubtedly react differently to different kinds of violence. And this reaction is not always easily predicted. For example, Poole (1983) has made the point that the rioting of the early years which was often accompanied by intimidation and property damage led to considerable population movement. People on both sides reacted by hurrying to reach the safety of their respective 'ghettos'. Later periods of violence, which often resulted not just in intimidation but in actual deaths, did not however have the same impact.

The response made by the authorities to the violence has also had its changing impact on the people of Northern Ireland during the last fifteen years. Again children have often unwittingly been involved in these creeping changes in Northern Irish society. The most obvious reaction on the part of the security forces to the violence has been twofold. First, to increase the size of the security forces on the ground and second, to arrest and imprison as many members of the paramilitary organisations as possible. Both these actions have implicated children in Northern Ireland.

In 1969 the police force in Northern Ireland (the Royal Ulster Constabulary – RUC) numbered about 3,000. As the troubles have escalated the size of this organisation has been increased to around 12,000. In addition, since then a locally recruited militia regiment of the British Army has been established, the Ulster Defence Regiment (UDR). So today almost 20,000 Northern Irish men and women are employed in the 'security industry' thus making them what the principal paramilitary organisation the Provisional Irish Republican Army (PIRA) calls 'legitimate targets'. Unfortunately these 'targets' mostly live in their own homes with their wives and children or with younger brothers and sisters. So today thousands of Ulster's children have literally been brought into the firing line of this apparently never-ending conflict. Similarly, the increased size of the security forces has meant that increasing numbers of men and women have been arrested and homes searched. Also, although the numbers of people charged with 'terrorist' type offences may only average around one thousand per year this, according to Hillyard (1983), is the tip of the iceberg. For example, he reports that from 1 September to 31 August 1978, 2,970 persons were arrested under the Northern Ireland Emergency Provisions Act but of these 1,900 were subsequently released. This means that for some children in Northern Ireland the sudden disappearance of a father, uncle or a brother has become a not unusual occurrence even if only for a short period of time. For many others of course daddy's disappearance may last a lot longer as Northern Ireland's prison population grew to a peak of 3,000 in 1978, although this figure is now beginning to fall.

Violence and the Everyday Life of Children

Even for those children not so directly involved security precautions have, in a host of little ways, touched their lives also. For example, the smallest child is now accustomed to the somewhat cursory bag inspection or body check on entering a large store. This is done in an attempt to prevent such items as miniaturised incendiary devices being smuggled in set to explode when the store is closed that night. In an attempt to halt car bombing city centres have been closed to private cars and in other areas 'control zones' established. These are areas where cars may be parked but never left unattended. So little Johnny or Jane have become accustomed to going along with dad or mum when they go to the city but staying in the car while their parents go off to the shops – a living symbol that their car at least does not contain a bomb.

But once again nothing stands still, and with the run-down in the bombing campaign control zones are beginning to disappear and in smaller towns at least motor traffic again is allowed in the shopping precincts. So marked has been this change that the words 'bomb scare' hardly mean anything to today's Northern Irish child where once they instantly signalled fear and alarm. This was in the 1970s, when the bombings were at their height, and the paramilitaries found that not only would the authorities have to pay attention to real bombs but an even cheaper form of disruption was simply to claim a bomb had been planted when it had not. Soon every public building, factory and even school had its plan for emergency evacuation. And soon school children discovered that one way to annoy school teachers and even to disrupt examinations was simply to dial the school's number and utter the words everyone dreaded hearing – 'You've got five minutes to get out.'

Fortunately those days, days spent standing in the rain in the playground while the school was searched, perhaps more than once in the same day, now seem to have passed. Although today bomb scares still happen they are less often malicious and more often deliberate acts of the paramilitaries or due to some 'suspect package' (as the security jargon puts it) which an absent-minded shopper has left behind. Still the point remains that in all sorts of ways the violence has touched the everyday lives of children in Northern Ireland. However, the way in which the violence has manifested itself has changed over the years and has varied from place to place and indeed from child to child.

The important point for the reader is that this must always be kept in mind even when researchers make the mistake of talking about 'the children of Northern Ireland' as if they were some homogeneous mass who all had in common the fact that they had been exposed to 'the violence'.

Conclusions

Understanding the way in which growing up in Northern Ireland may have influenced the children and young people of 'war-torn' Ulster is not a simple exercise. To begin with there is a shortage of information about children before the troubles began. And even since the violence flared up in 1969 research has been relatively slow to get off the ground. Part of the reason for this is that carrying out research in Northern Ireland is not an easy task, posing ethical problems for both respondents and researchers.

Added to these difficulties is the fact that researchers must try to take into account that the violence is only one of the problems faced by Ulster's children – the principal problem, it could be argued, is poverty. Sadly what makes children and young people in Northern Ireland unique is the fact that they live in a part of the world where violence exists, not that they may suffer from poverty or deprivation. And further difficulties for researchers arise because of the changing nature of this violence over the last fifteen years which means that not all children in Northern Ireland have been equally exposed to violence or even to the same kinds of violence. All of this means researchers face an enormous problem in teasing out the impact of the violence alone.

Undaunted, researchers both locally based and from other countries have increasingly risen to the challenge. The remaining chapters therefore will examine closely their work and conclusions. The next chapter begins by asking just how much have children in Northern Ireland been learning about the actual violence, have they become directly involved or indeed in the more peaceful areas are they actually aware of the violence going on in other areas? Unhappily some children have been only too well aware of the violence, ending up as casualties either physically or psychologically. Chapter 3 examines the evidence particularly related to the psychological stresses and strains imposed on Northern Ireland's young people and questions how they may have attempted to cope with this apparently never-ending burden. While these two chapters deal with fairly obvious consequences of growing up in Northern Ireland the next chapter (Chapter 4) looks at a more subtle consequence of violence in Northern Ireland, the way it may have influenced moral development ranging from actually committing crimes to attitudes towards institutions such as the schools and the churches.

The remaining three chapters focus rather more on the causes of the conflict itself rather than its consequences. Chapter 5 examines social-psychological explanations for the way in which the conflict apparently ensures that each new generation comes to identify with its own particular side thus ensuring that the conflict is carried on while Chapter 6 focuses particularly on the role of the divided school system in this process and the potential benefits of school integration. Finally Chapter 7 attempts to look into the future and to predict how the present generations of young people in Northern Ireland will behave politically in the years to come stressing particularly the conditions necessary if these young people are to emerge as future peacemakers rather than potential warmongers.

2

Learning about Violence

The history of modern Ireland is a catalogue of violence – both parts of the island, the Republic and Northern Ireland, owe their very existence to violence or the threat of violence. And unfortunately to the Irish, as Stewart (1977) has so aptly put it, all history is applied history:

> ... that is history they learn at their mother's knee, in school, in books and plays, or radio and television, in songs and ballads. (Stewart, 1977, 16.)

Nevertheless it came as a shock to the people of Northern Ireland – no less to the rest of the watching world – when the media revealed, in the early days of the troubles, that at least some children in Northern Ireland had learned their history lessons only too well and were applying what they had learnt in the streets of Belfast and Derry.

Involvement in Violence

At first this involvement in violence was confined almost exclusively to rioting in one form or another (although as time progressed the 'rioting' became less haphazard and more organised) and headlines such as 'Teenagers attack police in Belfast' or 'Bogside youths clash with British troops' became common. Children were reputed to be involved in burning homes and intimidation, and one writer (Fields, 1973) even went so far as to claim that children had become so expert in stone throwing 'over vast distances with great accuracy as to surpass adult athletes.' (Fields, 1973, 126).

The Report of the National Advisory Commission (1968) into the riots in the USA had reported that the typical American rioter in the summer of 1967 was an unmarried male between the ages of fifteen and twenty-four. Press reports of the early 1970s record that children as young as ten years were involved in rioting in Northern Ireland at this time and that some were actually arrested and charged with rioting offences. Nevertheless these children were the exception rather than the rule and an analysis of those arrested between May 1969 and April 1971 (Lyons, 1972a) revealed that of over 1,500 people arrested only about 15 per cent were nineteen years or younger, the vast majority of these being young men. There may of course have been a tendency, if not a policy, on the part of the army and police at this time not to arrest younger rioters but to concentrate on adults, assuming perhaps these were the riot leaders. Some suggestion of this comes from data reported by Mercer and Bunting (1980). Mercer and Bunting, instead of using official statistics on those arrested (after all only a small proportion of rioters at any time) simply asked about 800 adolescents (average age seventeen years) whether they had ever taken part in a demonstration. Of course, being in a riot and being in a demonstration are not the same thing. Nevertheless it could be argued that at this period in Northern Ireland one was often a forerunner to the other. Also young people were much more likely to respond honestly to questions about their participation in demonstrations than they were to being questioned about being in a riot (even on an anonymous questionnaire). And what Mercer found was that about a third of these young people admitted to having taken part in a demonstration. This incidentally is very similar to the figure obtained from a random sample of adults in the early 1970s (Boyle, *et al.* 1970). This suggests therefore that indeed rather more adults may have been arrested for rioting and that those figures therefore underestimate the number of young people who participated in riots. However, like the official statistics, Mercer's research revealed that more males than females admitted to having taken part in demonstrations and also more Catholics. Of the young males who responded to Mercer's questionnaire 47 per cent of the Catholics and 22 per cent of the Protestants indicated that they had taken part in a demonstration but for females the corresponding figures were lower at 25 per cent and 16 per cent respectively. Interestingly Mercer and his colleagues did not simply attempt to catalogue these facts but also tried to explain why these young people were motivated to demonstrate in the first place. Surprisingly they found few differences between those young people who had engaged in demonstrating and those who had not. For example, demonstrators were no more aggressive or tough minded, no more (or less) religious nor were they simply young people who could be labelled as sensation seekers. Instead it appears that demonstration participation was more likely to be linked to feelings of social powerlessness and normlessness and adolescent demonstrators were more likely to rate themselves as unhappy rather than happy. However, what Mercer's research could not explain was whether this unhappiness was due to personal reasons, or because of discontent with the Northern Irish political situation.

Gradually the pattern of violence began to change however and street confrontations between large numbers of people and the security forces became much less common. Unfortunately the changing pattern of violence and the movement towards greater use of the bomb and the gun did not end all children's or young people's direct involvement in the violence. To be sure, many fewer children were now involved but those children who were caught up in the violence were of course involved in a much more dangerous way. Obtaining hard facts about children's involvement with violence during this period is difficult for several reasons. First of all, not many social scientists were active at this time and those that were faced definite problems about obtaining hard data. Further, children's involvement in the violence at this time became something of a propaganda issue with the government suggesting that the paramilitaries were making use of children and literally hiding behind children on occasion to escape detection. Certainly, newspaper reports of the time suggest that more than once children were used to create a diversion while gunmen escaped. Indeed, children were even alleged to have been used as shields, placed between a gunman and the security forces.

If the interviews Fraser (1974), a child psychiatrist, reports verbatim with children at this time are to be believed then children were indeed very directly involved, for example to the extent of being taught how to make petrol bombs and even at times encouraged to use them. However, one must treat these reports with some caution. The temptation for an eleven-year-old boy to exaggerate the importance of his involvement in the violence of the time must have been enormous especially when Belfast was apparently filled with gullible adults only too willing to listen. Fraser's (1974) informant however strikes a note of truth when questioned about allegations that children were paid by older men to throw bombs:

> If they were paying, the whole street would be out. But they'd be wasting their money because we'd do it for nothing. (Fraser, 1974, 17.)

Unfortunately the information available in official statistics which indicates how many children and young people have been charged, over the years, with 'terrorist type' offences also suggests recruitment of young people and children by paramilitary organisations has been a particular problem. Indeed, Curran (1984), writing on 'Juvenile Offending and Political Terrorism', suggests that the data available indicate that the extent of young people's involvement in 'political terrorism' in Northern Ireland appears to be considerable. Curran presents figures for the years 1975, 1976 and 1977 for under-sixteens charged with various offences. These reveal that during this period seven under-sixteens were charged with murder and six with attempted murder while forty-one were charged with firearms offences and two with explosives offences. In the older age category, sixteen to eighteen years, these figures are virtually trebled! This information has been updated in a recent publication (PPRU, 1984) which provides information from 1978 to 1982. Unfortunately the information is not presented in exactly the same way as Curran's in terms of labelling of the offences committed nor are the age categories used exactly the same. Nevertheless the information provided by Curran (1984) and by the PPRU paper gives the impression that children and young people's direct involvement in serious violence increased steadily from 1975 to peak in 1978 when nearly one hundred young people in the ten to seventeen-year-old category were charged with such offences. These numbers then dropped dramatically to twenty-four in 1979 and have remained at that level, except in 1980 when only four young people were charged with 'terrorist type' offences.

Who Gets Involved?

Something of a controversy has however grown up concerning the type of children who have become involved in serious violence in this way. On the one hand there is the theory that these are innocent children who, had it not been for the 'troubles', would never have seen the inside of a courtroom or a police cell. For example, Taylor and Nelson (1977) reported that:

> teachers in training schools, and lawyers, for example, are often aware that political offenders frequently have no criminal record, come from impeccably 'respectable' homes and do not believe they have done 'wrong' – all factors distinguishing them from many of their non-political fellows in borstals or training schools. (Taylor and Nelson, 1977, 16.)

This idea has been challenged however by some empirical work in which young people on 'terrorist' charges have been compared with those charged with 'ordinary' criminal offences. For example, Elliott and Lockhart (1980) compared some forty 'terrorist' offenders with a matched group of non-terrorist offenders and reported some interesting differences. For example, the 'terrorist' offenders were older on average (sixteen years) compared to the comparison group (fourteen years). Perhaps more significantly the scheduled offenders (as they are technically known) were not just older but also more intelligent, had better educational attainments and were more socially outgoing. Prior to getting into trouble with the law they were also less likely to have been truants at school or to have been referred to a child psychiatrist. On the other hand the 'ordinary' delinquents and the scheduled offenders came from very similar backgrounds. Most (almost half) came from the lowest social-class, while about one-third came from one-parent families and in both groups some forty per cent had either a parent or, more likely, a sibling who had a criminal record.

A further study by Curran (1980) compared a group of juvenile 'terrorist' offenders and a similar group of juvenile delinquents, this time using a self-report measure, the Jesness Inventory. This consists of 155 statements to which the boys involved were required to answer either 'true' or 'false'. These statements were then used to provide five measures in terms of Social Maladjustment, Value Orientation, Alienation, Manifest Aggression and Autism. Curran (1984) reports that overall the results revealed 'a complex pattern of similarities and differences' between the two offender groups with the major differences being that the 'terrorist' offenders scored lower in terms of aggression, autism and value orientation (a measure of among other things toughness and sensation seeking). Once again therefore it appears that the young people convicted of 'terrorist'-type offences emerged with a rather better profile. Yet from these results it must be concluded that despite their superiority in various ways, the scheduled offenders do not come from such a different sub-culture that they would all have remained out of trouble with the law had it not been for the troubles. Rather it appears that some probably would have run foul of the law at some time but because of the troubles in Northern Ireland more young people there are becoming involved with the law and involved on much more serious charges (Boyle, Chesney and Hadden, 1976).

But why are the more intelligent, less aggressive young people more likely to become involved in paramilitary activities? One simple explanation may be that the paramilitary organisations, on both sides of the religious divide, only accept or recruit the more intelligent to their organisations. Or perhaps the more intelligent young people are more aware of what is going on around them and hence more likely to volunteer. For the moment however, just what makes a young person opt for political violence as opposed to ordinary crime must of course remain a matter of speculation.

This is because surprisingly little attention has been devoted to this question. Instead, as the story of Northern Ireland began to unfold, what really caught the imagination of the media and their viewers and readers around the world was not that children and young people were involved in serious violence but rather the tender age of some of the participants. Children as young as five and six years could be seen throwing stones, laughing, jeering and generally challenging the forces of law and order. Indeed, on some occasions, if reports are to be believed, children acted as if they were themselves responsible for law and order, redirecting traffic, setting up road blocks, stopping and questioning pedestrians. Even greater alarm was aroused when it was learned that children too young to actually take part in the violence were apparently involved with violence at least at a fantasy level, incorporating what they saw going on around them into their play activities. Thus according to newspaper reports one of the favourite street games of this period was 'playing riots'. An authoritative report, from the National Society for the Prevention of Cruelty to Children in 1971, stated that in play groups (where children were generally aged about four to five years) many of the children, especially the boys 'spend considerable time erecting barricades across the floor and pretending to shoot and throw petrol bombs.' Soon these verbal reports were being reinforced by photographs of children erecting street barricades or posing, toy gun in hand and dressed in quasi-military uniforms. It must be added however that according to rumour at the time, photographers who could not actually find children spontaneously behaving in this way were not above paying in order to get the desired picture.

Awareness of Violence

Despite all this journalistic interest in children's involvement in violence in Northern Ireland – or perhaps because of it – social scientists were slow to show a similar concern. In fact the first research paper in this area was not published until a study by Jahoda and Harrison appeared in 1975. Fortunately when they did become involved social scientists tended to show a healthy scepticism for the wealth of media reports by addressing first the fundamental question – are the children of Northern Ireland actually aware of the violence going on around them? What social scientists, particularly psychologists were interested in specifically was how much children's thinking and behaviour had been influenced by living in a violent environment. But first they felt it necessary to establish that the children themselves regarded their environment as a violent one. To do this Jahoda and Harrison chose to study children from two schools, one Catholic and one Protestant, located in an area of Belfast were the troubles had been greatest. The children were all boys, half aged six years, half aged ten years. Rather than ask children directly about the violence Jahoda and Harrison decided to adopt an indirect approach which involved presenting each child with a street made up of model houses. In this street were positioned four cardboard figures – a postman, a milkman, an 'ordinary' man and a soldier. Each child was asked to imagine he was walking along a street either in the (mainly Catholic) Falls district or in the (mainly Protestant) Shankill Road district. Four objects were then handed to the child one by one and the child was asked if he found this object in the street which of the people in the street would he hand it to. The objects were a cigarette packet, a letter, a milk bottle and a parcel. These were chosen because, while they are innocent everyday objects yet each had been used fairly regularly to make bombs in the early 1970s in Northern Ireland. Of course this was precisely what the investigators were interested in; how would these Belfast children regard a parcel, a milkbottle, etc. – as harmless everyday objects or as potentially lethal weapons of urban guerrilla warfare? Jahoda and Harrison therefore simply recorded the number of children who perceived one or more of these objects as a bomb and these results were compared with those from a similar group of children who carried out exactly the same task but who lived in Edinburgh in Scotland.

And their results showed that while almost one third of the thirty six-year-old Belfast children identified at least one of the four objects as a bomb, only one of the thirty six-year-olds from Edinburgh did so. Similarly 80 per cent of the ten-year-old Belfast children identified at least one of the objects as a potential bomb compared to only two of the Scottish children. As the authors noted, the fact that even six-year-old children were beginning to learn to treat ordinary everyday objects as sources of danger was in itself an eloquent testimony to the kind of world in which these children were growing up, and could in fact be regarded as an appropriate adaptation to the reality of life in Belfast in 1973.

This study can of course be criticised on several grounds. To begin with it is rather limited in scope involving only a small number of children from a geographically very restricted area of Belfast – some would say an area not typical of Belfast as a whole let alone Northern Ireland. Perhaps the most important criticism that could be levelled at the study is that the children may have been cued, that is unwittingly encouraged, to give the sort of 'bomb' responses the investigators were looking for. Particularly the fact that the people in the street included a policeman and a soldier plus the fact that the children were told that the street was located in an area of Belfast notorious for violence at that time. Nevertheless this study did include one very important feature which had been missing from the earlier media reports and unfortunately missing even from some subsequent academic studies in this area. That is the inclusion of a comparison or control group – a group of children from an area outside Northern Ireland (in this case Scotland). Only the inclusion of a group like this alongside the responses of children from Northern Ireland permits an investigator to say if children in Ulster are in some way different with regard to what they have been learning about violence.

Fortunately this study by Jahoda and Harrison has been followed by others which have also involved a control or comparison group from outside Northern Ireland. And the next study which was carried out in 1976 (Cairns, Hunter and Herring, 1980) went some way to overcoming the criticism that the materials presented to the children were perhaps suggesting violent type responses. This time the children, who were all aged five to six years and were living in either a virtually trouble-free part of Northern Ireland or in a south London suburb, were presented with ten line drawings of scenes such as a train crash or a derelict house. Each picture was accompanied by a standard question requesting an explanation for the scene depicted and the child's response recorded. Again a count was made of the number of children mentioning bombs or explosions at least once. This revealed that while some 20 per cent of the London children mentioned bombs or explosions 90 per cent of the Northern Irish children did so. Again however this study was limited in scope comparing only twenty children from one small town in Northern Ireland with twenty children from London.

This study was therefore repeated one year later, in 1977, as before involving five to six-year-olds from a trouble-free part of Northern Ireland compared this time to a similar group of Scottish children (Cairns, *et al.*, 1980). And once more the results suggested greater awareness of bombs and explosions among the Northern Irish children (45 per cent) as compared to the Scottish children (4 per cent). Overall therefore the results of both these studies reported by Cairns *et al* (1980) are in broad agreement with the results obtained by Jahoda and Harrison (1975) roughly three years earlier. More children in Northern Ireland it seems are aware of Northern Irish type violence compared to children in other parts of the British Isles, and this holds, it would appear regardless of whether these children live in the ghettos of Belfast, at the very heart of the conflict, or in the quieter rural parts of Northern Ireland. This latter finding is particularly intriguing and is one which will be returned to later.

Northern Ireland is of course not the only part of the world today where children may be exposed to violence. An interesting question then is are children in Northern Ireland any more or less aware of the violence in their country compared to children in other countries which have also experienced violence? This is the question Hosin and Cairns (1984) tried to answer in a study carried out during 1979-80. The children were somewhat older than those in the earlier studies being either nine, twelve or fifteen years of age and this time information was again elicited indirectly, by asking them to write, in not more than ten minutes, a short essay entitled 'My country'. Approximately 200 children at each age level took part in this study, with equal numbers from either a society which (at the time of the study) was directly involved in a conflict (Northern Ireland and Jordan) or from a society on the fringe of a conflict (Iraq and the Republic of Ireland). In order to find out if children in the 'violent' societies really were aware of the conflict in their country the essays (a total of 2,785) were searched for any reference to violence – for example mentions of shooting, killing, bombs, guns, etc. What is of interest here is that at virtually every age level more children from Northern Ireland mentioned violence at least once in their essay (34 per cent at nine years, 70 per cent at twelve years and nearly 90 per cent at fifteen years). In all 66 per cent of Northern Irish children mentioned violence at least once compared to 30 per cent from the Republic of Ireland, 19 per cent from Jordan and 7 per cent from Iraq. Once again this is evidence that children in Northern Ireland are well aware of the violence in their society. But this time there is also the suggestion that the kind of violence experienced in

Northern Ireland – urban guerrilla warfare – may have a bigger impact on children than even out and out warfare with another country such as that as experienced by the children in Jordan.

The surprising feature of this last study is that not only were the Northern Irish children apparently the most aware of violence but that these children did not come from areas in Northern Ireland where the violence had been worst. Does this mean that all children in Northern Ireland are equally aware of the violence in their country? Or does it mean that the children in the most troubled areas are somehow more aware or at least have a more detailed knowledge of violence? And regardless of which of these alternatives is true, how did the children in the more peaceful areas learn about the violence going on elsewhere, especially children as young as five or six years? These are the kinds of questions social scientists in Northern Ireland have now begun to tackle.

The answer to the question as to whether children in the more peaceful parts of Northern Ireland know more or less about the troubles (or are more or less aware of them) has turned out to be neither a straightforward yes nor a straightforward no. This is illustrated in a series of studies reported by McIvor (1981). In the first of these (Taggart, 1980) 192 Catholic and Protestant children, aged five, nine, and twelve years, were selected from two towns, one that had experienced a considerable amount of violence and one that had been relatively peaceful. Each child was then presented with two unfinished stories and asked to supply an ending. The stories of course were deliberately designed so as to be ambiguous in a Northern Irish context. In other words they were capable of being interpreted in terms of Northern Irish violence or in an ordinary everyday manner. The first story in fact referred to boys throwing stones and the second to the discovery of a discarded parcel outside a shop. The most interesting feature of the results was that there was no difference in the number of children interpreting these stories in terms of Northern Irish violence in the 'quiet' town and the 'violent' town. There was however a tendency for older children to provide more 'troubles' related endings to the stories and for more children (24 per cent) to interpret the parcel story in this way (that is suggesting it might be a bomb) compared to the stone throwing story which provoked a troubles related ending from only 1 per cent of the children.

McIvor (1981) extended this study by repeating more or less the same procedure with 120 children (all Catholics) this time living in a violence prone area of west Belfast. Once again children were more likely to interpret the stories in terms of the troubles as they got older but this time 45 per cent saw the stone throwing incident and 38 per cent the parcel story in Northern Irish terms. In other words, looking at the results over both studies it appears that the parcel story called to mind a possible bomb in about a third of the children – regardless of whether they lived in a high violence area of Belfast, a high violence rural town or a relatively trouble-free town. The stone throwing story, however, meant something special only to children from west Belfast. The most obvious explanation for this is that bombs have been a feature experienced by many more parts of Northern Ireland and also explosions have always been well reported by the media. Stone throwing as a violent political act has however been less common, confined largely to the two main cities of Northern Ireland – Belfast and Derry – and has attracted little media interest. It is not surprising therefore that detailed knowledge about the violence or awareness of specific forms of violence could vary from location to location. In general terms however this research suggests that children in Northern Ireland, regardless of where they live, appear to be equally familiar with the violence.

This differentiation between specific and general knowledge about the violence has been illustrated in further studies, this time using the technique of asking children to write essays. In the first of these (McIvor, 1981) nearly 1,000 children aged seven and eleven years from violent and less violent areas in Belfast were asked to write an essay entitled either 'Belfast' or 'Where I live'. The most important result was that when the essays were examined for references to Northern Irish violence no differences were found between the high and low violence areas, with as many children in each area (about 45 per cent) alluding to the troubles. McWhirter (1982) carried out a somewhat similar exercise only this time the focus was more closely on the troubles *per se* because this time the children were asked to write an essay simply entitled 'Violence'. Again the children (637 aged nine and twelve years) came from a troubled area (in Belfast) and a relatively peaceful rural town. McWhirter's (1982) study differs from McIvor's however in that she made a particularly detailed study of the responses given by the children in their essays. This showed that although the children from both areas were well aware of the Northern Irish context of violence, they did differ to a certain extent in terms of the specific types of violence they wrote about. In particular children in the troubled areas mentioned five specific violent acts more often than did the children from the more peaceful areas; these were writing slogans, shooting, stealing cars, riot-ing and stoning police. Once more these are all activities more likely to occur in the violence prone urban areas of Belfast than in a more rural setting.

The Role of Television News

The surprising outcome of all these studies is not of course that the children from the more violent area have a fairly detailed knowledge of the troubles but rather that the children from the quieter areas are, comparatively speaking, so well informed on this topic. The next ques-tion therefore is how are the children in the peaceful parts of Northern Ireland learning about the violence? Two obvious sources are first adult conversations and second the media – particularly the television news. The television news, rather than other forms of news reporting, is a likely source because while children, especially young children, do not read newspapers very much (and yet are aware of the violence), they may well see the television news. Of course, five-year-olds do not usually settle down in their favourite armchair to watch the news but they undoubtedly are exposed to it accidentally. Also the television news because of its predominantly visual nature is likely to have a bigger impact than say the radio news. Certainly, some reports from the earlier days of the troubles had mentioned children's preoccupation with the television news. For example, it was reported that in the early 1970s children rioting in the streets, usually in front of a barrage of TV cameras from around the world, made sure they always got home in time to enjoy their own performance on the early evening television news. To appreciate the potential impact of television news in Northern Ireland one has to realise of course that coverage of violence there by the local news organisations has been almost one hundred per cent. To people in other parts of the world it may seem that violence in Northern Ireland has been over-reported. In fact, reporting outside of Northern Ireland has been fairly selective (Elliot, 1976). Today only 'outstanding' acts of violence in Northern Ireland appeal to the world's media. In North-ern Ireland itself however, it appears the media have felt an obligation to report virtually every incident however trivial. This has meant that at times when the level of violence has been particularly high a ten or fifteen minute local newscast could consist almost entirely of a 'string of violent episodes' (Blumler, 1971) with little or no contextual material. For example, in 1976 over a one month period the word 'bomb' was used on average twice per bulletin in the BBC's national newscasts from London while it was used eight times per bulletin in the same month on the BBC's local Northern Irish newscasts from Belfast (intended only for viewers in Northern Ireland).

Surprisingly, despite the massive amount of attention that has been paid to the possible influence on children of fictional violence on television, very little research has examined the impact on children of the real-life violence shown daily on the television news. One reason for this may be because early studies in the USA (Lyle and Hoffman, 1972) suggested that very few children choose to watch the news on television, especially younger children. Indeed, the opinion was that children could be said to be actively averse to the television news. However, as usual it was probably a mistake to translate findings from the USA into an Irish setting. This is because in the USA there are many more television channels to watch and indeed more television sets in the home. It is undoubtedly easier therefore for children in the USA to avoid being exposed to the television news. Not so in Northern Ireland, where only a small number of channels is available and most houses contain only one set, a set which is usually to be found in the main family room. Under these circumstances avoiding television news is a much more difficult process. Indeed preliminary research by Cairns and his colleagues (Cairns, 1981) had suggested that whereas American research (based on children's self-reports) had reported that about 30 per cent of children almost never watched the television news, in Ireland the comparable figure was about 5 per cent.

With this evidence in mind the present author undertook a series of studies to examine the role of television in informing children in Northern Ireland about the violence occuring in their country. The main difficulty in such research was of course that children who are exposed to Northern Irish television news are exposed to the Northern Irish media generally and also to adult conversations. Fortunately however Cairns, Hunter and Herring (1980) were able to find a group of children who were more likely to be exposed to Northern Ireland television news broadcasts only. This was possible because at the time the research was conducted (1976-7) certain parts of Scotland's west coast could receive television only from a transmitter situated in Northern Ireland. In other words, children who were not actually living in Northern Ireland were nevertheless being exposed to Northern Irish regional television news broadcasts. These children (from two different locations in western Scotland) were compared with another group actually living in Northern Ireland and with a third group living in Scotland but not exposed to Northern Irish news broadcasts. In all locations the children were aged either five to six years or seven to eight years. The younger children were shown drawings of such things as a train crash and a house on fire and were asked to say what had happened, while the older children were asked to write a short essay which was to begin 'Here is the news. . .' A simple word count based on the words 'bomb' or 'explosion' was carried out on the younger children's stories and the older children's essays. This revealed that the children who lived in Scotland who could not see Northern Irish television virtually never mentioned bombs or explosions. On the other hand, one third to half of the children living in Scotland but exposed to Northern Irish television used these words, particularly at the older age level. The essays in particular revealed that children living in a relatively remote, almost idyllic location in western Scotland were well aware of the tenor of local Northern Irish news broadcasts, writing such things as:

> There has been a bomb in Belfast it killed sixty people and it injured thirty people. Good night.

and:

> A bomb let off in Belfast yesterday and it exploded four houses. . . .

or, perhaps most aptly:

> A bomb has just gone off in Belfast and that is the end of the news.

What do the initials RUC and UDR stand for? Where are the Falls Road and Crossmaglen? What is a Control Zone? These are some of the questions, in multiple choice format, which Cairns (1984) presented to children in the next set of studies examining the possible role of television news in informing children about the violence in Northern Ireland. Direct questions such as these were employed this time because it could be argued that the word counts of the earlier studies provided at best only a crude index of awareness as opposed to knowledge about violence. The study involved nearly 500 eleven-year-olds who lived in five different parts of Ireland, chosen because they could be thought of as forming a rough continuum along the island of Ireland of increasing distance from where the actual scenes of violence took place. All completed this eleven-item multiple choice questionnaire and also indicated how often they saw the television news; 'frequently', 'sometimes' or 'never'. Overall the results showed that those children who watched the television news more often knew more about the troubles than did those who were not frequent news viewers, again implicating the television news as one possible source of children's knowledge about the violence. Also, the closer children lived to the actual scenes of violence the higher they scored on the test. Surprisingly however the children from the most northerly town only scored at a slightly higher level (6.86 out of eleven on average) than did those in the town situated on the southern-most tip of Ireland (5.55).

Another odd aspect of these results was that although television as suspected was obviously a source of knowledge about the violence for children, it was apparently acting equally to inform children who lived close to the violence and children who lived far away from it.

One possible reason for these quirks in the results of the first study was that the northerly town though closer than all the others to Belfast and Derry had itself been relatively trouble-free. Perhaps what is important is psychological distance from the troubles not geographical distance. To test out this idea a further study was completed in 1982. This time approximately 600 children took part at two age levels – eight years and twelve years. The children were selected from five different towns, all of approximately the same size. One of these towns was again in the extreme south of Ireland but the remaining four were in the north of Ireland – two in separate areas where the level of violence has been below average and two in areas where the violence has been above average. Again the children completed the questionnaire which contained the eleven-item multiple choice test dealing with the troubles and again they were asked how often they saw the television news. Once again among the eleven-year-olds those who watched the news frequently knew more about the troubles than did those who watched it less frequently. But this effect did not obtain at the eight-year-old level, where news viewing behaviour was not related to knowledge about the troubles.

However, the most important result in the present context is that the children who lived in the two 'quiet' towns scored at exactly the same level as the children who lived in the two 'violent' towns. Once again this suggests that, at least where constant features of the violence are concerned, children in quiet and violent areas of Northern Ireland appear to be equally knowledgeable. Of course, once more children who lived in Northern Ireland scored at a higher level than did children who lived in the Republic of Ireland. Finally, an interesting aspect of these results is that in this most recent study the difference between children in the north of Ireland and the Republic was much more marked than it had been in the first study. More remarkable still the mean score for eleven-year-old children from the Republic was almost exactly the same in both years (1979 and 1982). The mean score for children at this age level in the north had however increased from around 6.8 to 8.5. It is not clear how much stress should be laid upon this increase but certainly it appears to lend some credence to the suggestion that children in the north may be steadily increasing their knowledge about the troubles over time.

The Violence: in Perspective?

Having established that children in Northern Ireland are indeed aware of the violence going on in their country the next important question is: have the children got the violence out of perspective? After all many of these children, the evidence suggests, depend upon the media as a main source of information about the violence. And as noted earlier, the media image of Northern Ireland is of a land of perpetual violence and nothing but violence.

Happily, the evidence available to date suggests that children in Northern Ireland have not been influenced by media coverage of 'the troubles' in this way. For example, both McIvor (1981) and Hosin (1983) report that violence is not usually the first thing that comes to children's minds when asked to write about 'where I live' or 'my country'. Many children do mention the violence of course, but just as many also mention things such as the geography of Northern Ireland or the climate (Hosin, 1983). So Northern Irish children do not appear to think of their homeland as a place noteworthy only because of the violence going on there. Similarly, children appear to be sensitive to the fact that all parts of Northern Ireland are not equally caught up in the violence. This came to light when Cairns (1982) asked children in two relatively high violence towns and in two relatively low violence towns whether there had been 'much trouble' in their district in the last three years (the children answered on a four-point scale 'none', 'little', 'some', 'a lot'). Only 27 per cent of the children from the two 'quieter' towns thought 'some' or 'a lot' of violence had occurred in their district compared to 46 per cent from the more 'violent' towns (an interesting question of course is why this figure was not 100 per cent, a point taken up again in Chapter 3). This seems to suggest that despite possible exposure to a daily diet of Northern Irish violence in the media children, happily, have the violence rather more in perspective than might have been expected.

This observation is reinforced by a further study by McWhirter, Young and Majury (1983). They had the interesting idea of investigating Northern Irish children's knowledge about the causes of death. In order not to make too much of an issue of the question these investigators simply added the word 'death' (or 'dead' for younger children) to the end of a standard vocabulary test in which children are asked to give the meanings of words. Over 200 Belfast children were individually questioned in this way ranging in age from three years to fifteen years. Having explained what the word meant to them the children were then asked some additional questions about experience with death and about the causes of death. And it was this latter question that produced the most fascinating result because it revealed that overall death was attributed more often

> to sickness than to accidents *or* violence. On a more specific level, just as many children cited heart disease or old age as explosions or shooting and more children ascribed death to road accidents and cancer than to violence related specifically to the Northern Irish conflict. In short, the children's perceived realities quite accurately reflect the objective situation. (McWhirter *et al.*, 1983,91.)

Conclusions

Despite journalistic enthusiasm for the proposition that violence must have touched the life of every single child in Northern Ireland, social scientists have approached the topic in a more cautious fashion. This caution has been partly fuelled by the knowledge that many of the children of Northern Ireland live in parts of the province virtually unaffected by the violence.

Careful research carried out over the last ten years has however suggested that indeed the majority of children in Northern Ireland almost certainly are well aware of the violence going on around them and that this applies equally to children who live in the unscathed areas and to those who live in city ghettos. Local variations are of course to be found in terms of detailed knowledge about specific forms of violence peculiar to, for example, urban rather than rural locations – such as street rioting. But by and large the evidence is that as children get older, they become increasingly knowledgeable about the general features of Northern Irish violence.

This widespread dissemination of knowledge about violence among children in Northern Ireland, it has been suggested, may be due to two particular aspects of the Northern Irish conflict. First there is the fact that it is a 'guerrilla' based conflict rather than a conventional war. This may well mean greater awareness on the part of the population in general, and perhaps particularly on the part of children in comparison to children whose country is involved in a conventional war. The second and related aspect is the intense local media coverage of the violence and especially coverage on the part of that medium most readily accessible to children – the television news.

Yet despite all this exposure to violence – either directly or indirectly – the evidence is that children in Northern Ireland have not become totally overwhelmed by the troubles. That is they have not absorbed Northern Ireland's media image to the extent where the very names 'Northern Ireland' or 'Belfast' conjure up nothing but thoughts of death and destruction. Indeed, despite the media concentration on violent death in Northern Ireland children have apparently been able to retain a perspective which allows them to understand that in most years since 1970 more people in Northern Ireland have died in road accidents than have died as a result of the 'troubles'!

Given then that children in Northern Ireland are in general relatively well informed about the violence the next question is what impact has the violence had upon these children, either directly or indirectly? Again this has been a subject of much speculation – often ill-informed speculation – since the troubles began. The next chapters will therefore examine the evidence that has begun to accumulate on this topic, in an attempt to decide if the early prophesies of growing moral disintegration and mounting psychiatric casualties among young people in Northern Ireland have indeed come to pass.

3

Victims

Bombs Kill Children Too

Mention the impact of violence upon children in Northern Ireland and what immediately springs to mind is the psychological impact of violence on children. However, before going on to examine this popular and relatively well researched topic it is necessary to remember what people appear to have forgotten, that the violence in Northern Ireland kills children too. Perhaps this is something that people want to forget. It has been said that the greatest taboo subject of our modern technological age is death, particularly the death of a child. Maybe this accounts for the apparent lack of interest in the physical impact violence has had on children in Northern Ireland.

Another possible explanation for the lack of interest in this topic is the difficulty in obtaining information about the child victims of violence. Indeed, despite the fact that the Northern Irish conflict is perhaps one of the most intensely reported, most closely studied conflicts ever, no one knows exactly how many children have died, how many have been maimed, and how many injured. Murray (1982) has estimated that between 1969 and 1977 some 103 people under the age of seventeen years have been killed (or 8 per cent of the total) while the present author estimates that between 1969 and 1983 some 150 children under fourteen years have been killed or injured. These latter figures are at best however 'guestimates'. The reason for this lack of hard data is, first, that official statistics do not give a breakdown of victims in terms of age (or indeed in terms of sex or religion). The only other possible source is press reports. But here, as indeed with official statistics there are particular problems. Often, for example, a victim may be identified as a schoolboy or a schoolgirl without an exact age being given. A headline therefore that states 'Schoolboy shot in murder bid' could mean that a five-year-old has been shot or an eighteen-year-old. Yet another difficulty in compiling statistics in this area is deciding whether a child has really been a victim of the troubles or not. And finally there is perhaps the most sensitive issue of all, at least as far as local reporting is concerned, that is the question of attributing blame.

All these problems are well illustrated when one attempts to examine what information is available on children who have been killed and injured over the course of the last fifteen years. For example, even deciding who exactly the first child victim was is not a simple task. Was it, as some would claim, the five-year-old girl killed in February 1971 when she was knocked down by an army vehicle? Or was she simply the victim of a simple everyday traffic accident? Such accidents were of course by no means rare, particularly when at one time thousands of British troops, plus their vehicles (many of them gigantic armoured personnel carriers with restricted vision for the driver) were crowded into the narrow streets of Belfast and Derry. If this child was not the first victim then that dubious honour must fall to the seventeen-month-old girl who, in that phrase which so well describes the position of children in Northern Ireland was, in September 1971, 'caught in crossfire' during an attack on an army patrol in Belfast. This incident illustrates the problem involved in deciding who to blame for such deaths.

Was this the fault of the army for opening fire when children were nearby, or was it the fault of the IRA for attacking the army in the first place? A sterile argument it could be suggested, yet one which on many occasions has generated much heat in Northern Ireland, particularly where the deaths of children have been concerned.

Typical of this search for blame perhaps is the case of Brian Stewart. Brian was thirteen years old when he was shot in the head by a rubber bullet. He died six days later. At the time the army claimed he was part of a rioting mob which attacked a foot patrol of soldiers. Local residents however claim that when Brian was shot no rioting was going on. Since then his mother, aided by the National Council for Civil Liberties has been urging the European Human Rights Commission to find that the British Government was in breach of the human rights convention by using rubber bullets (now replaced by plastic bullets) as riot control weapons. Once again this is not an isolated incident, several children have been killed or injured by rubber or plastic bullets often in contentious circumstances. Sadly, this case also illustrates another fact of life in Northern Ireland. And that is that in most cases, victims of the violence, be they adults or children, are soon forgotten by all except their immediate family. Only those children whose deaths in some way became a *cause célèbre*, such as Brian Stewart, are still remembered today.

Of these perhaps the most remarkable is a child who can undoubtedly claim to be the youngest recorded victim of the Northern Irish conflict, a victim before her life even officially began. Cathy Gilmore was still in the comparative safety of her mother's womb when in July 1976 she became another statistic of the Northern Irish troubles, with a bullet lodged in her tiny body. Luckily both she and her mother survived and she was born a month prematurely as her mother was treated for her injury. Two days later she was operated upon and the bullet was successfully removed. Cathy then spent the next nine months of her life in hospital, five of them in an incubator. Three years later she was awarded £8,000 compensation after protracted legal arguments as to whether she was really a 'person' or not at the time she was wounded (*Times*, July 2, 1981). The last press report of her in 1981 indicated that she was alive and well and still living in Belfast.

This incident, apart from its uniqueness, illustrates a sad feature of the circumstances surrounding the death or injury of many of the child victims of the troubles. Many became victims when they had most reason to expect to be secure, for example in their own homes (many in their own beds), victims of a bullet meant for someone else, perhaps another member of their family. Similarly, many children have been killed while actually in the presence of their parents, blown to small pieces for example by booby trap bombs intended to kill their policemen or soldier fathers and often planted overnight in the family car designed to detonate on the ride to school.

It could be argued that the people of Northern Ireland have, over the years, of necessity, become hardened to violent death which no longer has the same impact as it once might have had. However, it would appear that the violent death of a child can still help to stimulate feelings of revulsion for violence and longing for peace. This has been particularly evident in that two anti-violence movements in Northern Ireland have originated with the deaths of children. The first is an organisation known as Witness for Peace which was started by the Reverend Joseph Parker whose son was killed on 'Bloody Friday', a day in Belfast in 1972 in which eleven people were killed by simultaneous bomb explosions. Sadly the Reverend Parker has now left Northern Ireland to live elsewhere and his organisation has declined into obscurity. The second organisation to begin in this way was the Peace People, once an internationally acclaimed peace movement whose founders were awarded the Nobel Peace Prize. This organisation originated from an incident in which the Maguire family's three children (including a four-week-old baby) were killed by a car which was out of control because the driver had earlier been shot by security forces who were pursuing him. The deaths of these three children began a chain reaction of peace demonstrations which spread across both communities in Northern Ireland in the single biggest popular movement for peace that Northern Ireland has so far experienced. Sadly, this movement is now also almost defunct.

Sources of Stress

For every child who has been killed or injured in the troubles there have been many more who at some time must have felt their life was threatened and more still who have had to witness the horror of death or injury inflicted upon others. Often the other has been a close friend or relative. This is because as the pattern of violence has changed slowly but surely over the years, deaths and injuries have resulted less from street rioting or even bomb explosions and more from single acts of assassination. Many of these assassinations have taken place at the victim's place of work or, more often, in his (most victims have been men) own home. As a result hundreds of children in Northern Ireland have had to witness their father's murder. For example, according to press reports, the most recent assassination victim at the time of writing had just seconds before his death been holding his three-year-old daughter in his arms. On another occasion a whole classroom of elementary school children watched as their school teacher was gunned down and on more than one occasion school bus drivers – easy targets in the rural areas where they are employed – have been similarly dealt with in front of their young charges.

Not a lot of information is available about children who have been indirectly victimised in this way either by being forced to witness terror at first hand or by themselves being terrorised. Researchers are obviously sensitive to the fact that such children may, for some time, be in a delicate psychological state which probing or questioning could easily exacerbate. However, some information is available though often obtained by indirect means. For example, McKeown (1973) in the course of a survey of all post-primary schools in Northern Ireland asked the question, 'Has there been any harassment of pupils on their way to and from school?' Over 70 per cent of the 255 schools polled responded and of these 51 per cent reported that indeed such harassment had occurred. In fact forty-eight schools reported assaults on pupils including fifty seriously injured and one child killed.

Nor has harassment simply been confined to children coming and going to school. The most serious form of harassment during the early 1970s was centered around the place where children have the most right to feel safe – their home. With the outbreak of street violence at the beginning of the troubles many families found themselves living in the 'wrong' area – that is in an area where, in religious terms, they were in a minority. In this situation these families often became scapegoats for the intensely felt anger of the time. Thus 'intimidation' as it became known was for a time one of Belfast's most serious problems. This phenomenon has been graphically described by Darby and Morris (1973), who explain that in many cases intimidation took the form of actual physical violence. Children or sometimes pets might be attacked, mothers or fathers beaten or jostled, eggs, stones, petrol bombs or bullets directed through windows or doors, homes ransacked, furniture piled up in the streets and burned and in some cases the actual houses themselves were burnt down. In other cases threats were simply used perhaps in the form of anonymous letters or phone calls or slogans were painted on walls. More subtle intimidation might take the form of neighbours becoming less friendly, for example refusing to talk to housewives at the shops, not allowing children to play with their friends and so on.

The result of all of this was what Darby and Morris (1973) have described as 'the largest enforced population movement in Europe since the Second World War.' During the period August 1969 to February 1973 they estimate that somewhere between 8,000 and 15,000 families moved home as the result of intimidation. In other words, somewhere between 30,000 to 60,000 people were forced to leave their homes in the Greater Belfast area alone. Many of these refugees were children and Murray and Boal (1980) in their research attempted to focus specifically on families with children who moved home because of intimidation. To do this, they compared those households with children who moved home between 1969 and 1972 either because of intimidation or for other more normal reasons. Of the 353 households in their study about one third had moved because of intimidation, broadly defined. Of these intimidated families the majority (66 per cent) had moved because of direct attack or threat either to their home or members of their family. The remaining households in the group indicated that they had moved simply because of the general level of violence in their area. And if the results of this survey are representative then they suggest that children may have accounted for well over half of those forced to flee their homes at this time. This is because, while only 10 per cent of the 'ordinary' households had four or more children, 35 per cent of the intimidated families fell into this category. Further, the intimidated households, particularly those directly threatened, were more likely to be single-parent families and also more likely to be working-class families with younger children. Additionally while 'ordinary' movers tended to remain within the same local area within Greater Belfast, and therefore presumably closer to schools, family and friends, the intimidated more often than not were forced to move to another district often Murray and Boal (1980) noted, not even adjacent to their original district. Thus for the intimidated, due to a combination of having younger children and the great distance moved, a change of school was more often involved. Finally, and perhaps not surprisingly, the mothers of the families that were forced to move were more likely to express dissatisfaction with their new environment than did the mothers from the other families.

Despite the fact that Murray and Boal (1980) were demographers and despite the fact that they had no direct evidence about the psychological state of children of the families forced to move, they could not resist commenting that:

> It seems that even if, despite all that happened to them before their flight, the children of the intimidated families have suffered no long-term psychological disturbance (a highly optimistic and probably untenable assumption) the circumstances of the move and its aftermath may give rise to further problems. (Murray and Boal, 1980, 30.)

And their concern reflects a general concern on the part of many naive observers at this time, not just for children forced to move house, but for all the children of the province. How people wondered, could children possibly survive unscarred the experience of seeing their homes burnt down, seeing their friends wounded, seeing their fathers arrested in the middle of the night or gunned down in the family home? Also less dramatically but perhaps just as stressful, thousands of children (*see* Chapter 2 for further details) have had to wait each night to see if daddy came home safely or not.

The Psychological Casualties

The first professional to report, from first hand experience, on the psychological wounds inflicted on children by the violence in Northern Ireland, was Maurice Fraser. In the early 1970s he was working as a child psychiatrist in the Belfast Child Guidance Clinic, itself almost literally only a stones throw from the narrow streets in which much of the early violence occurred. His book *Children in Conflict* is written in a frankly journalistic style and encompasses a wide range of topics not always strictly germane to the title. The two best chapters however are those which deal with children's psychiatric disorders and the violence – the subject after all one would expect a Belfast child psychiatrist to know most about. In the first of these chapters entitled 'Ten children' Fraser describes ten case studies of children whose psychiatric symptoms were precipitated by violent events related to the troubles. These were not a random sample of children undergoing psychiatric treatment in Belfast at this time; instead they were selected by Fraser and some bias may well have crept into that selection. Nevertheless this is a uniquely useful source of information about such children precisely because of its humane, non statistical treatment of the child casualties of this time.

Perhaps typical of these children, who as Fraser notes differ in specific details and yet present an overall pattern of reactions which is strikingly similar, was thirteen-year-old Margaret. Margaret was referred to a child psychiatrist because of fainting fits and what Fraser describes as symptoms of gross anxiety. We learn that she is the second of seven children all living at home, her father permanently unemployed. The child herself, we are told, has always been a shy and timid girl and is of limited intellectual ability. Her parents admit to having been very 'tense and edgy' since the outbreak of the troubles. This is understandable because during the riots of August 1969 several homes around them were totally destroyed while they themselves suffered intimidation and looting losing most of their belongings. This meant that they had to move into short-stay temporary accommodation and, while there, this area too became the scene of some of Belfast's worst violence with rioting several nights in succession. This rioting was not simply confined to the street but the parents reported on several occasions actually spilled over into their front garden.

The first time this happened Margaret 'screamed, fell, lost consciousness and had to be taken to hospital' where all physical investigations proved negative. However, though she was discharged from hospital and the rioting died down she continued to have fainting fits both at home and at school. These fainting attacks continued for some months sometimes precipitated by loud noises or other times by voices raised in anger or even simply by hearing reference made by her parents to the local political situation. On one occasion a fainting attack occurred after she had heard an explosion at a nearby quarry. On another, when a recent shooting incident was mentioned in her presence.

Margaret's history is typical in many ways. To begin with she is a girl, and of Fraser's ten children seven were girls. Secondly, she had a history of being a somewhat timid and fearful child before her illness occurred. Another common factor is the lack of emotional security in the home. Many of the ten case histories mention that either one or both of the parents were of a nervous disposition or perhaps were even undergoing psychiatric treatment themselves. The age range of Fraser's child victims was narrow, falling between eight and thirteen years. Fraser suggests in fact that from eight years to puberty children were most vulnerable. Younger children he suggests did not fully understand the danger of what was going on around them – a mother could explain away explosions by saying it was just thunder and younger children would be reassured in this way and hence not suffer unduly. Older children, Fraser suggests, were more likely to find refuge in action or in flight, perhaps becoming directly involved in the violence in their locality or, alternatively, leaving the area or even leaving Northern Ireland altogether. It was the children in the middle group therefore who were most likely to fall serious psychiatric victims to the violence. Finally, Fraser's ten children share one further common feature. This is that they not only suffered at the time of a particular violent incident (often in the form of fainting fits, or asthma attacks or sleep disturbances) but more seriously these symptoms continued long after the precipitating event. Indeed, in virtually all of the case studies Fraser presents these symptoms became worse with the passage of time, not better.

One has to remember, of course, that Fraser's observations are confined to children referred for specialist psychiatric treatment and in the earliest years of the violence only. Fortunately Fraser's work has been updated by McCauley and Troy (1983) in a paper in which they examine, in a rather more statistically-oriented fashion, the impact of conflict and violence on children referred to a child psychiatric clinic in Belfast. Their approach was to examine the psychiatric records of children referred in the years 1968, 1972, 1976 and 1980.

The first interesting fact to emerge from McCauley and Troy's data is one which initially seems rather surprising. This is, that the smallest number of child psychiatric referrals occurred in the year 1972 when 229 children were referred compared to a total of almost 400 in the other three years examined (1968, 1976 and 1980). As 1972 was the year when rioting and civil disturbances were at an all time high in Northern Ireland one might have expected referrals of children to a psychiatric clinic also to have peaked at this time. How can this be explained? One possible explanation is that this is an artefact due to changes in referral patterns. All children seen by a psychiatrist have to be referred by some other agency, usually the family doctor. If these agencies adopt different criteria in different years to select children for referral then the number of referrals may also change from year to year. Indeed, children not only have to be referred by their family doctor to the psychiatrist but before that can happen the family doctor has to be consulted by the child's parents. It is possible therefore that this chain may have broken down at some point under the stresses and strains of communal violence.

On the other hand it is possible that these figures do represent the true state of affairs – that is that fewer children became psychiatric victims in 1972 and therefore fewer were in need of specialised psychiatric services. This explanation does appear at first glance to fit in with what is known about trends in adult psychiatric illnesses at this time. This is because a series of studies conducted in the early 1970s concluded that there was no evidence of any increase in psychiatric illnesses among Belfast adults which could be attributed to the violence common at this time (Lyons, 1971). Actually it has been claimed that if any change in levels of adult psychiatric illnesses were detectable during the early 1970s these changes represent not an increase but a decrease. For example, Lyons (1972) has documented a decrease in the incidence of depressive illness in Belfast city during the period 1969-70. Similarly, Lyons (1972b) has presented data for suicide rates in Northern Ireland over the period 1964-70 which reveal a mean decrease from 86.7 cases per year for the period 1964-69 to a total of 48 cases for the year 1970. Seen against this background McCauley and Troy's data may thus be seen as charting the same phenomenon in child psychiatric illnesses and could therefore reflect a true decrease in psychiatric illnesses among children severe enough to warrant referral to a psychiatrist.

McCauley and Troy (1983) not only examined gross figures for psychiatric referrals in the four years they sampled but also carried out a detailed examination of the case notes of a random selection of the children referred during those years. In most cases this amounted to roughly a one in three sample. These case notes were then examined and information extracted with regard to such things as the diagnosis that was eventually arrived at, the family background and, of particular interest here, whether the 'troubles' were actually mentioned in the case notes. Over all four years the sample of children (average age about ten years) consisted of more boys than girls (three out of five) mostly living with their natural parents. One out of every four of the children had recently moved house and in one in twenty of the cases one of the parents had had a personal psychiatric consultation. When the case records were examined for mentions of the troubles the interesting fact that emerged was that in 1972 and 1976 about 30 per cent of the records contained at least one such mention. In 1980 however this dropped to 12 per cent, that is eight out of the 109 cases examined. These references to the troubles were then further classified as either a general anxiety – for example about living in a troubled area – or a more specific concern with the child or family being closely concerned with or actually involved in a specific event such as a bombing or shooting. When this was done a difference emerged between 1972 and 1976. Not surprisingly in 1972 general anxieties were more prevalent (72 per cent) but this had dropped (22 per cent) considerably in 1976. In other words, in 1976 and in 1980 when the troubles were a factor worth noting in a child's psychiatric history it was more likely to be because of a specific event such as an explosion or killing. This is exactly what one would expect from a knowledge of the changing pattern of the violence over these years. Thus these data presented by McCauley and Troy (1983) help to put Fraser's (1974) limited, but more intense observations into their proper perspective. In particular they remind us that the children he described so vividly were, thankfully, largely children of their time.

Unfortunately, in attempting to understand the extent of any health problem information from specialist services – such as psychiatric services – does not provide a complete picture. To begin with there is as noted earlier the problem that everyone who is seriously ill will not necessarily be referred to a psychiatrist. Therefore, as McCauley and Troy (1983) note it is quite possible that children who were just as ill as those that were referred to their clinic were never actually seen by a psychiatrist but were helped by other agencies, some of which have grown up as a result of the troubles. They cite as an example of one such organisation the counselling service offered to families of injured or deceased police personnel by the police welfare service.

Nevertheless, as McCauley and Troy (1983) point out, the clinic from which they obtained their data provides a regional assessment, consultation and treatment service for the whole of Northern Ireland's psychiatrically and psychologically disturbed pre-school and school-aged children. Therefore, one must assume it is to this clinic that the majority of psychiatrically disturbed children in Northern Ireland would have been referred. This makes it all the more remarkable that a gross discrepancy is apparent if one compares the number of children referred to the clinic from the Belfast area and estimates of the number of psychiatrically disturbed children supplied by Fee (1980, 1983) on the basis of survey research. McCauley and Troy (1983) indicate that from the Belfast area about 240 children were referred in every year they examined, except 1972 when the figure was 153. This is very much smaller than the estimate arrived at by Fee (1983) which was about 500 in 1975 and 286 in 1975 – just for eleven-year-olds in Belfast alone. Fee obtained his information by asking the teachers of Belfast primary school children (some 5,000 in 1975 and 7,000 in 1981) to complete for each child a questionnaire specially designed to detect psychiatrically disturbed children – the Rutter Teacher Questionnaire (1967). Rutter has suggested that about 60 per cent of the children classified as 'disturbed' on this questionnaire would normally be confirmed as disturbed when examined by a psychiatrist and it was this figure that enabled Fee to make his estimates. Of course, one would not expect these proportions to apply to every age band and no doubt in choosing to survey eleven-year-olds only Fee chose one of the age groups most at risk for psychiatric disorder and hence produced slightly inflated figures. Nevertheless, even allowing for this, Fee points out that if his figures are correct 'this means that several thousand children of school age may be regarded as seriously disturbed in Belfast' (Fee, 1983, 56), a very different figure from the 200 plus children from Belfast referred for specialist psychiatric assessment. On the other hand, Fee's data do agree with McCauley and Troy's in that they suggest a decrease in the number of psychiatrically disturbed children over the period 1975 to 1981.

Despite this, the gap between McCauley and Troy's figures and the estimates provided by Fee is puzzling. Indeed, this gap is wider than at first appears. This is because a certain number of the children referred to specialist psychiatric services will usually turn out *not* to be psychiatrically ill in the strictest sense of that term. This is in fact reflected in the data provided by McCauley and Troy (1983). Particularly in 1972 and again in 1980 over one-third (35 per cent) of the children were classified as having 'no abnormality'. The important point here is that this does not mean that these children were not suffering in some way; rather it means as McCauley and Troy point out, that the disorder may not have been sufficiently marked or prolonged to cause handicap to the child or his or her parents. Children like this, that is with mild or transient disorders were therefore classified as exhibiting no abnormality.

Of course the majority of such children, that is those with mild or transient disorders, would not be referred to a psychiatric clinic and we can probably safely assume that those recorded by McCauley and Troy were simply the tip of the iceberg. Indeed, Fraser (1974) is on record as suggesting that by far the most common problem, in the early 1970s at least, was that of acute emotional reaction to the violence experienced by children who lived in riot areas. That is children suffered psychiatric symptoms such as those described earlier but these symptoms diminished as soon as the streets became quiet. In this context it is interesting to note that Fraser suggests that based on accounts he obtained from parents, teachers, clergymen and indeed children themselves 'that scarcely any child living in riot conditions has escaped at least some symptoms of acute anxiety.' (Fraser, 1973, 84). Perhaps the explanation for the difference between McCauley and Troy's figures and Fee's estimates is therefore that it is largely these children that the questionnaire used by Fee is detecting. Also one must remember that whether these children are indeed 'psychiatric cases' in the strictest sense or rather suffering a short-lived disorder, their suffering is nonetheless all too real.

However one cares to label the children Fee's research is particularly interesting because it allows comparisons to be made between his data gathered in Belfast and roughly similar information gathered in two other areas in Britain. This comparison is possible because Rutter carried out two earlier studies using the same teacher questionnaire only this time with ten-year-old children, first in the Isle of Wight and then with a sample of children from ten Inner London boroughs (Rutter, Cox, Tupling, Berger and Yule, 1975). Comparing the results of Fee's earlier Belfast survey, which is obviously closest in time to Rutter's research, some interesting facts emerge. Perhaps the most important of these is that the incidence of disturbance in Belfast children (15 per cent) was recorded as higher than that for children in the Isle of Wight (11 per cent) but lower than Rutter's estimates for children in Inner London (19 per cent). In other words, the Belfast results came out as one would have expected. Fee therefore concluded that despite the one year difference between the samples the incidence of disturbed behaviour in Belfast, as far as the school system is concerned, is probably no worse than might have been expected in similar urban areas in other parts of the United Kingdom. (Fee, 1980, 42).

Yet while the overall rates for disturbance among children appeared to fit in with Rutter's data some divergence did occur. In particular it emerged that children categorised as 'antisocial' were relatively more common than were those categorised as 'neurotic' in the Belfast results. Further, this trend was especially marked in the Belfast girls' results compared to the London girls' results. As Fee notes one possible explanation for this phenomenon is that it is in some way related to the violence in Northern Ireland which somehow 'caused neurotic behaviour to be "displaced" by antisocial behaviour' (Fee, 1980, 41). Unfortunately when Fee (1983) described the results of his second 1981 survey he did not maintain this distinction between antisocial and neurotic disturbance in the detailed figures he presents but simply noted that by far the largest proportion of children who could be described as disturbed fall into the antisocial category.

Fee's work provides a wealth of information because not only did he use it to compare rates of disturbance across geographical areas and across time but also across the Northern Irish religious divide. This is possible because his survey included schools attended almost exclusively by Protestant children (controlled schools) and those attended exclusively by Catholic children (maintained schools). To his surprise Fee found marked, statistically significant differences in his 1975 data between Protestant and Catholic subjects. Further, these differences were tempered by the sex of the child to the extent that more Protestant boys (17 per cent) were rated as 'antisocial' than were their Catholic counterparts (10 per cent). Similarly more Protestant girls (6 per cent) were rated as 'neurotic' than were their Catholic peers (2.4 per cent).

This was a rather unexpected result and one which is difficult to explain particularly when the fact that more of the Catholic children came from poorer homes is taken into account. The most likely explanation is that the Catholic/Protestant divide was confounded by or confused with some other factor. The fact that such confounding may have occurred inevitably raises questions about the overall quality of Fee's data. This is because, in the end, the decision to regard a child as disturbed or not was based on a particular teacher's rating of that child. Admittedly at the primary school level children usually only have one teacher in any one year and therefore that teacher has plenty of opportunity to get to know his or her children really well. The weakness however is that no check is made to see that all the many teachers involved are using the same criteria to rate the children. Therefore, what one teacher regards as antisocial behaviour could be seen as quite unremarkable behaviour by another teacher. Further, what a particular teacher regards as antisocial behaviour might not only depend on his/her personal ideas about children's behaviour but upon the general standard of the children's behaviour in the school in which the teacher is working. In other words, local school-based 'norms' could easily have influenced the way teachers rated children in Fee's research. And this is important in the context of Catholic/Protestant differences because these schools often differed in at least two other ways besides the fact that they were attended by children from different religious denominations. These two differences were (Fee, 1983) that the Protestant schools were more mixed in social class terms and also were mixed in the sense that the pupils consisted of both boys and girls. Catholic schools on the other hand were more likely to be stratified in socio-economic terms, according to Fee (1983) and more likely to be single-sex schools. Both these differences could of course have meant that the local school norms for what constituted disturbed behaviour may have varied enormously.

One way to get around this problem is not to ask the teachers about the children's behaviour but to ask the children directly about themselves. This, according to McWhirter (1983a), is a much less problematic approach to the problem of measuring psychological adjustment in children and one which she therefore adopted. The questionnaires she chose to use were two well-known standard pencil and paper tests for children – one developed in England, the other in the USA. The English test was the Junior Eysenck Personality Questionnaire (JEPQ) which claims to measure three independent personality factors – 'extraversion', 'neuroticism' and the oddly named 'psychoticism' best thought of as tough-mindedness. A fourth scale on the JEPQ is referred to as the lie scale and is included to detect malingering or careless responding. The American questionnaire was the Spielberger Trait Anxiety Inventory for Children (STAIC) which claims to measure the same personality factor as the neuroticism scale of the JEPQ.

These two questionnaires were completed by some 1,000 children from Northern Ireland. These children were chosen so as to represent two age levels (ten years and fourteen years) and also contained approximately equal numbers of Protestant and Catholic boys and girls. In addition about half the children came from a part of Belfast which had experienced violence relatively frequently while the remainder came from three more peaceful rural Northern Irish towns. As well as the Northern Irish children McWhirter also included a sample of approximately 270 children from Manchester in northern England in an attempt, as she says, to discover how 'troubled' children in Northern Ireland might be compared to children living outside Northern Ireland. All the Manchester children were fourteen years old and completed the same questionnaires as the Irish children. The information gained from these questionnaires enabled McWhirter (1983a) to compare the performance of the Northern Irish children in two ways. First it was possible to compare the fourteen-year-olds with the same aged children from Manchester. Second it was possible to compare the responses of the Northern Irish children with the test norms for both the JEPQ and the STAIC. This is because when both these tests, English and American, were being developed they were completed by very large numbers of 'normal' children in their respective countries.

Comparing the results of the ten-year-old Northern Irish children with those of the original standardisation group revealed that on the JEPQ the Northern Irish boys emerged as very slightly more tough-minded than their English counterparts and scored lower on the lie scale. Also they scored at a slightly lower level on the anxiety scale than did the original American sample. Similarly, the ten-year-old Northern Irish girls also emerged as slightly more tough-minded and lower on the lie scale. In addition however they scored somewhat higher on the neuroticism scale of the JEPQ. Of particular interest here is the fact that when McWhirter (1983) compared the ten-year-old Northern Irish children from the 'peaceful' areas with those from the 'troubled' areas she found that both boys and girls from the more violent area scored at a significantly higher level in terms of tough-mindedness. Similarly, Protestant boys scored at a higher level than did Catholic boys on the tough-minded scale but no such difference emerged where girls were concerned.

These results are particularly interesting in that they echo some of the findings noted above produced by Fee's (1980) attempts to investigate the same problem using very different methods. Especially if one equates the psychoticism or tough-minded scale of the JEPQ with Fee's antisocial category then both pieces of research appear to be suggesting that Northern Irish, or perhaps more correctly, Belfast children are rather more tough-minded than are English children. Once again the suggestion is that Protestant children, or rather Protestant boys at least, are more tough-minded/antisocial than are Catholic boys. And not only has McWhirter apparently replicated Fee's findings but she has extended them by suggesting that this higher level of tough-mindedness may be a correlate of the environment in which a child is living, to the extent that children from more troubled areas present themselves, on the JEPQ at least, as more tough-minded than do children from more peaceful areas.

Surprisingly, the same comparisons carried out on the questionnaires completed by the fourteen-year-old children in McWhirter's study revealed none of these differences. This time two comparison groups were involved – the test's normative sample and McWhirter's own Manchester sample. Nor at this age level did she find any differences between children from 'troubled' and 'peaceful' areas nor indeed any differences between children from differing religious persuasions. This is puzzling and given the fact that the results from the ten-year-olds fit in so well with earlier findings it is difficult to decide why the fourteen-year-olds' results did not follow the same pattern. Two explanations may be suggested, the most obvious being that by age fourteen years children have learned to produce the answers to questionnaires that are expected of them. That is, they present themselves in a more favourable or socially desirable light and hence are less likely to admit to such things as enjoying a practical joke that could sometimes really hurt people, an item from the tough-minded or psychoticism scale, or indeed to the fact that they would not be upset to see a dog that has just been run over, another item from that scale. However, examination of the average scores suggests that this is unlikely to be a correct explanation because ten-year-old Northern Irish boys and fourteen-year-old Northern Irish boys responded positively to equal numbers of the 'tough-minded' questions. It may well be, therefore, that this is a true reflection of a real phenomenon and that, for some reason, Northern Irish children – to put it simply – grow up rather more quickly than do children in England – at least in terms of being tough-minded. The fact that McWhirter (1983a) reports that her ten-year-old children from the 'troubled' area were more tough-minded than those from the peaceful area, suggests that environment indeed may have a role to play here. Further, it should be noted that even the children from the peaceful area in Northern Ireland appeared to score more highly on tough-mindedness compared to the English normative group. Of course, whether one regards being tough-minded as a sign of disturbance in children is highly debatable. As McWhirter (1983a) observed, comparing McCauley and Troy's results with Fee's, tough-mindedness or antisocial behaviour is obviously something that concerns school teachers more than psychiatrists.

The other interesting aspect of McWhirter's study is that in terms of the earlier information available from Fraser's (1973) observations and the data gathered by McCauley and Troy (1983) and Fee (1980, 1983), nowhere do her results suggest that thousands of children in Northern Ireland may be thought of as being disturbed in the 'neurotic' sense. In other words, her results indicate that both in terms of the neuroticism scale of the JEPQ and in terms of the American anxiety scale (STAIC) Northern Irish children do not appear to be any more neurotic/anxious than their English or North American counterparts. Can we therefore conclude from this information that indeed Northern Irish children are no more 'troubled' than are children elsewhere? Of course, McWhirter's data were gathered in a later time period than most of the earlier research and therefore it could be that her results simply reflect the trend noted by both McCauley and Troy (1983) and Fee (1983) of a gradual decrease in the number of child psychiatric victims. Nevertheless, while this seems a reasonable explanation it cannot be accepted without reservation. This is because it is debatable whether the questionnaires McWhirter used really measure what a psychiatrist would label 'neurotic illness' or a teacher would rate a 'neurotic disturbance' in children. What the JEPQ neuroticism scale and the STAIC anxiety scale really measure is whether a child has what could be described as a neurotic or anxious personality. In other words, is the child basically an anxious type of person. This of course is different from saying that a child is in an anxious state such as might require treatment by a psychologist or psychiatrist, but rather says something about a constant feature or personality trait ascribable to that child.

Fortunately the JEPQ and STAIC were not the only measures related to anxiety that McWhirter obtained from the children in this study. A second paper (McWhirter, 1984) reports that she also asked the children to complete a 'stress events rating scale' and to write a ten minute essay entitled 'The Worst Day of my Life'. Unfortunately it would appear that all the children completed the stress events scale immediately before they wrote the essay. This is unfortunate because items on the stress-events scale may have cued the children to write about particular topics. For this reason the information from the stress-events scale is probably more valuable and will be the main focus here.

The stress-events rating scale consisted of twenty-six events which children might possibly find stressful. The majority of these were ordinary events such as going to the dentist, nightmares, moving school, scary films, plus some other rare but relatively common events such as the death of a parent, thunder and lightning, being sent to the principal. Nine of the events however were such that they could either directly or indirectly be considered as related to the violence in Northern Ireland – for example bomb scares or getting caught in a riot. The children were asked to consider each item and then respond on a four-point scale from 'an awful lot' to 'a little' how much they would find such an event troublesome or worrying.

All of the children both in Manchester and in the Northern Irish violence prone and peaceful areas completed the stress-events scale except that four of the items, relating to Northern Irish type violence were not considered appropriate for the English children. Comparing the overall score from the stress events scale (that is the score averaged across all the events rated by the children) within the Northern Irish group only, revealed some statistically significant differences. These differences appeared to be related particularly to the age and religion of the children involved. That is ten-year-old children perceived the events as more stressful than did the fourteen-year-olds and similarly the tendency was for Catholic children to perceive the events as more stressful than did Protestant children. Strangely whether the children lived in a troubled part of Northern Ireland or not, did not have a clear effect.

When the Northern Irish children's results were compared with those from the Manchester sample no differences emerged in terms of overall mean score on the stress events scale. This result was confirmed when McWhirter (1984) examined the individual items on the stress events scale. This she did by rank ordering the items in terms of their mean rating (rating ranged from 1.19 to 3.73 with most grouped around the middle point of 2.5) from most stressful to least stressful. When this was done separately for the Northern Irish ten-year-olds, the Northern Irish fourteen-year-olds and the Manchester fourteen-year-olds then the most obvious fact was that the three or four items seen as most stressful were almost identical on each of the three lists. In fact all three groups placed 'parent being killed' as the most stressful followed by either 'parents fighting' or 'having an operation'. Also at the least stressful end of the scale there was a fair degree of agreement with 'violence on TV' figuring in bottom place for two of the three groups. It is also perhaps surprising that for the Northern Irish children at least some of the Northern Irish troubles related events – such as 'soldiers on the street' or 'getting stopped at checkpoints' – appeared near the very bottom of the list. That is Northern Irish children did not perceive these as particularly stressful events.

Of course, such events as seeing soldiers on the street or being stopped at a checkpoint may be relatively frequent events in a Northern Irish child's life. McWhirter (1984) therefore felt these data allowed her to conclude that children in Northern Ireland have built up a certain amount of resilience to the violence and indeed may have become 'habituated' at least to certain features of the violence in Northern Ireland. This seems a reasonable hypothesis based on what is known to date. But can it therefore be concluded, as McWhirter appears to do that Northern Irish children are not exposed to undue stress and thus are not at risk in terms of becoming psychiatric casualties. The problem is that what McWhirter has gathered information about, using her stress events scale, is how children in Northern Ireland (and Manchester) *perceive* potentially stressful events. What this does not reveal, however, is how often the children had actually been exposed to such events. This is important because despite the fact that the children in Northern Ireland and Manchester did not differ in their perception of the amount of stress associated with particular events, if the Northern Irish children had experienced a greater number of these events in their lifetime then it could be that the cumulative effect might have had potentially disastrous consequences. This therefore is the information that is now required in order to make a proper assessment of the amount of stress that children in Northern Ireland have been and indeed are being exposed to. Here it must be hastily added that it was not Mc-Whirter's (1984) fault that this vital information was not obtained. She in fact points out that she originally intended to measure the children's experience of the events but had to remove this element from the study 'due to objections from some school principals'. Unfortunately, yet again, an example of the problems researchers must face in the sensitive climate of Northern Ireland. Depite this omission (if it can properly be labelled an omission) McWhirter's study has broken new and valuable ground and can be used as the basis of future studies in this area which will further extend our understanding of the possible psychological stresses and strains life in Northern Ireland may impose on children.

The latest investigators to provide further valuable information in this area are McGrath and Wilson (1985). This research is particularly valuable because not only does it provide more information but, more especially, it extends the range of the existing work to embrace children outside the greater Belfast area – the sole focus of virtually every other investigator to date. McGrath and Wilson, in a study involving nearly 600 randomly selected ten to twelve-year-olds included among their battery of tests a questionnaire designed to measure depression which was completed by the children themselves plus the Rutter Scale completed by their teachers. And what they suggest, in a preliminary report of their work, is that the effects of the troubles may, by the late 1980s, be compounded by the severe ecomonic situation prevailing in Northern Ireland leading, they suspect, to much higher levels of self-rated depression among Northern Irish children compared to a similar English sample.

To the naive reader it might appear that we now possess a vast amount of information about children's psychiatric reactions to the stress associated with exposure to the violence in Northern Ireland. Unfortunately, in this area, as in others, even today we do not really have enough information to reach a clear understanding of such simple facts as how many children have really become psychiatric victims solely because of the violence. On the other hand the information we do have, meagre as it is, does fit neatly into a pattern of similar results from other countries and at other time periods. And the information reviewed above concerning children in Northern Ireland allows us cautiously to reach the following conclusions: first of all, it is apparent that when the violence was more intense, particularly in the form of street rioting, more child psychiatric casulties resulted; secondly, at this time and indeed in succeeding years, the majority of children who have suffered psychologically because of the violence have experienced this trauma for relatively intense but short-lived periods of time and have apparently recovered quite quickly.

The overall picture therefore, while incomplete, is that a small proportion of Northern Ireland's children have suffered terribly and for long periods of time. A larger proportion have suffered less severely and for a much shorter time, but perhaps more surprisingly to the outside observer, the vast majority of Northern Ireland's children have apparently lived through the violence without becoming psychiatric casualties. This is exactly the sort of overall result one would predict based on earlier studies such as those involving children exposed to the blitz in wartime England (e.g. Bodman, 1941) which reported that the majority of children did not break under the strain. And this finding has been replicated more recently, also in war-time conditions, in studies involving children exposed to shelling during fighting in Israel (e.g. Ziv *et al.*, 1974). In turn, the fact that the Northern Irish results agree with those involving children from other parts of the world, exposed to similar sorts of stress, allows us to place a certain amount of faith in the Northern Irish research, inadequate as it is.

Coping with Stress

On the other hand what none of the earlier research nor indeed the work done in Northern Ireland reveals is – how this was possible. How did the majority of children exposed to violence or threats of violence manage to emerge relatively unscathed? This is an important question, not just for academic reasons but for very practical reasons. For example, if it is known why certain children are vulnerable it may be possible to identify those who are most at risk. And if it is known how most children survive intact then it may be possible to use this information to help the vulnerable children become less vulnerable.

It is therefore worth considering for a moment how children in Northern Ireland may have avoided the debilitating effects of stress. No research aimed at answering this question has as yet been carried out in Northern Ireland, although it is becoming a major area of interest to researchers throughout the world (Rutter, 1983). Nevertheless the research literature on Northern Ireland does contain some hints as to the processes involved. For example, Fraser (1974) claimed that he had observed that vulnerability was related to three main factors. First, the degree of emotional security the child enjoyed both before and during the stressful event – this emotional security, he notes, was related not only to the child's own psychological resources but particularly to those of his or her immediate family. A second important factor was of course the stressful experience itself. Finally, Fraser draws attention to the important fact that a child's response to stress is to a certain degree unique and depends upon his or her own usual way of responding to new experiences (Fraser, 1974, 99). Fraser has therefore identified two areas which may be usefully explored further, the emotional climate surrounding the child as provided by the child's immediate family, and the child's individual style of coping with stress.

Surprisingly, given the unsubstantiated claims about the strength of the family in Ireland, remarkably little seems to be known about contemporary Irish family life which would help support Fraser's observations. What is definitely known about families in Northern Ireland is that the typical Northern Irish family is rather larger (about 2.2 children per family) compared to that in the rest of the United Kingdom (1.8). Further, not only is a Northern Irish family less likely to be a one parent family but also a child in Northern Ireland is more likely to have at least one parent who is not working (PPRU Monitor, 1984). However, apart from relatively superficial facts such as these not much is known in detail about Northern Irish family life. Indeed, it appears that only one study (Whyte, 1983) has been published which investigates family life at all in Northern Ireland. Fortunately this one study took the perspective most relevant to this discussion – that is how family life in Northern Ireland may have played a role in enabling children to cope with 'the troubles'.

Whyte (1983) simply asked twelve-year-old children in either a Catholic area of west Belfast, a Protestant area of east Belfast and an inner city suburb of London to report on such things as 'who decides what you can watch on TV' and do you normally do such things as wash your hair, take a bath etc. on your own or switch off your own light at night and decide which clothes you wear. The surprising result that Whyte obtained was that the greatest control by parents was exerted by Catholic parents in west Belfast. However, this marked control was not applied equally to all Catholic children but particularly to Catholic boys. That is boys in Catholic west Belfast seemed to be more under the control of their parents compared to boys in the other two areas and even compared to Catholic girls. At first glance this is a rather surprising result but it may well tie in with Fee's (1980, 1983) observation that teachers reported fewer children in Catholic schools were, in their opinion, prone to indulge in antisocial behaviour. Similarly it also fits in with an earlier finding by Curry (1983). Curry asked Catholic and Protestant mothers in a relatively quiet rural town in Northern Ireland to estimate the average age at which children should be able to carry out certain tasks by themselves ranging from feeding themselves to taking a job without first asking parental permission. Overall Catholic parents tended to set a higher average age for these activities. Taken together the evidence produced by Whyte (1983) and

Curry (1983) could be indicating that Catholic parents in Northern Ireland adopt a more protective attitude towards their children. Why this is so must of course remain something of a mystery awaiting the outcome of further research. One obvious possibility is that this is a response on the part of Catholic parents to the environment in which they are bringing up children in the Northern Ireland of the 1980s. Catholic areas are more likely to be areas where violence has occurred (Poole, 1983) and indeed paramilitary organisations are more active in Catholic areas. This latter fact may well explain why Catholic parents in west Belfast may be keeping an even closer eye on their sons than are the parents of Protestant boys in east Belfast or the parents of boys in an inner London suburb.

Of course, it may not simply be that families have been, in some way, protecting Northern Irish children but rather that the children themselves have developed ways of coping with their atypical environment. At the moment two possible coping processes have been suggested – habituation and denial. Of these habituation is undoubtedly the simplest. Mercer, Bunting and Snook (1979) appear to have been the first people to suggest that in Northern Ireland 'people are adaptable and apparently can eventually get used to this nearly wartime environment.' More recently this has been echoed by McWhirter (1983b; McWhirter and Trew, 1981) who in an apt phrase has suggested that for Northern Ireland's children 'abnormality has become normality.' In other words, children in Northern Ireland have become so used to violence (or reports of violence) and its associated problems that for them it has become a 'normal' feature of everyday life. McIvor (1981) has claimed to have produced evidence to back up this idea. She asked students, not natives of Northern Ireland, to describe their impressions of the place on first arrival. A year later the same foreigners were asked to repeat the exercise. And a year later 'mentions of violence had almost disappeared from their impressions. Instead they concentrated on the more normal aspects of life' (McIvor, 1981, 8). Thus McIvor concludes that they had during the course of a year 'adapted, learned to cope or habituated to the conflict situation.' And this evidence might be highly acceptable clinching the debate in favour of the habituation hypothesis had not McIvor added one last sentence to her report: '. . . though they usually did complain about the abnormal amount of rain.' Could it be that these students had habituated to the violence but not to the rain? Obviously further work is required in this area and certainly McIvor's idea of a longitudinal study is the ideal way to investigate this whole question.

McIvor also presents evidence to suggest that denial may be a possible coping process used by children in Northern Ireland. In the course of one of her studies she had asked children from the same parts of Belfast to write essays entitled either 'Belfast' or 'Where I live'. The former title she noted had elicited many more mentions of troubles-related phenomena. One possible explanation for this, she suggested, was exposure to media coverage which had simply led children to associate 'Belfast' with violence. However, a second possible explanation she considered was that this was evidence of some kind of cognitive distancing from the troubles. To illustrate this she quotes a seven-year-old from what she describes as a particularly well-known trouble spot as saying 'there is trouble in Belfast but the trouble is downtown, way over the other part of town.' The fact that this child was apparently denying that his was a troubled area McIvor (1981) notes could be one way of adapting to one's situation – a way of coping.

Further evidence for the possibility that such a denial process may be at work comes in a study by Cairns (1982). He repeated to children a question that had first been asked by Russell (1974) in the period 1970-71. The question was 'Has there been much trouble in your district in the last three years?' The interesting result obtained by Russell was that on a scale from 'no trouble' through 'a little trouble' and 'some trouble' to 'a lot of trouble', more primary school boys chose the latter category (24 per cent of Protestants and 34 per cent of Catholics) than did the older secondary school boys (16 per cent and 11 per cent respectively). Unfortunately between asking the question of the older children and moving on to the younger children a definite escalation of violence occurred in Northern Ireland, following the introduction of internment without trial in 1971. This makes it difficult to say if fewer older children really perceived less trouble in their district compared to younger children. Nevertheless Russell's result clearly indicates that the majority of children, young and old, in 1971-72 were not prepared to endorse the 'a lot of trouble' response. This in itself is surprising. After all the violence had really only been in full swing for slightly over a year. Does this mean the majority of children in Northern Ireland habituated or got used to the violence in such a short period of time? Certainly if habituation is the explanation then children questioned in later years, it could be suggested, should show even more reluctance to claim that a lot of trouble had occurred in their area – both because actual levels of violence were now lower and because these children had had a longer period of time in which to habituate or become accustomed to a background of violence.

It is clearly of interest therefore that when Cairns (1982) asked the same question again of children in Northern Ireland he obtained virtually the same results as Russell had almost ten years earlier. The study carried out by Cairns differed slightly from that of Russell however. Instead of obtaining a sample which represented all children in Northern Ireland, Cairns (1982) chose around 100 children from each of two towns where violence was at a relatively low level (Poole, 1983) and two where violence – at least in terms of deaths per thousand of the population – had been relatively more common. Once again the results indicated that more younger children (seven years) were prepared to say that 'a lot' of trouble had occurred compared to older children (eleven years). This difference was particularly marked in the 'quieter' towns where on average 15 per cent of the seven-year-olds but only 7 per cent of the eleven-year-olds endorsed the 'a lot' category. This compared to 33 per cent and 21 per cent respectively in the 'more violent' town. Once again therefore this could be interpreted as indicating that fewer older children perceive there to have been a lot of violence in their district even when, by Northern Irish standards, their district is particularly violence prone. Further, even in these violence prone towns at most only one-third of the children perceived their district as experiencing 'a lot' of trouble. In other words, in 1981 as in 1971 the majority of children in Northern Ireland did not claim that there had been 'a lot' of violence in their district.

Obviously there are various ways in which this information can be interpreted but one is that at least some of the children questioned in both 1971 and 1981 were denying that a lot of violence had occurred in their area. Further, the indication is that this denial process may be more common in older children than in younger children. And these results have assumed a new significance due to the recent publication (Cairns and Wilson, 1984) of a study in which the same question was asked of adults. This time the question was asked in 1983 of about 400 randomly-selected adults in each of two towns, the towns again being chosen to include a high-violence town and a low-violence town. Remarkably, very few adults in either town endorsed the 'a lot' response when questioned about the level of violence in their district and indeed rather fewer did so in the 'violent' (0.5 per cent) as compared to the 'less violent' (3.5 per cent) town. Therefore, as with the children the majority of adults denied there had been a lot of trouble in their district even when the statistics on violence told a different story. However, Cairns and Wilson's (1984) study strengthened the denial hypothesis by revealing that those who perceived 'a lot' of violence also reported more psychiatric symptoms, but only if they lived in the more violent town. In other words, paradoxically those people who lived in a high violence town in Northern Ireland but denied that it was a high violence area reported that they suffered the smallest number of psychiatric symptoms. Once again more research is needed in this area, particularly research with children which replicates the Cairns and Wilson (1984) study. In the interim however it would appear that a convincing case may be building up that denial is indeed at least one of the important coping mechanisms being used by both children and adults in Northern Ireland.

Conclusions

Although very little hard information is available there is reason to believe that over the years a considerable number of children have become physical casualties of the violence in Northern Ireland, with perhaps as many as 150 deaths in the under-fourteen age group.

Strangely much more attention has been devoted to the question of whether children in Northern Ireland have become psychiatric casualties of the violence. And certainly children in Northern Ireland have been exposed to potential sources of stress. In the early years of the troubles these consisted largely of rioting or gun battles, happening perhaps right on the child's own doorstep or around him or her at school. In the early 1970s this caused a great many families to flee their homes thus probably adding to the stress and strain on children at this time. More recently, witnessing a father or a teacher gunned down has become a more common though less frequently occurring potential stressor while less dramatically (but more frequently) simply waiting to see if daddy comes home safely each night or indeed if daddy is the man referred to in the newsflash – 'reports are coming in of a policeman shot earlier tonight. . .' – must all place continuous strain on large numbers of children.

Quite a bit of evidence is now available on how children reacted to such stresses and strain. This evidence has come from widely varying sources such as individual case reports made by psychiatrists, ratings supplied by teachers reporting on the psychological health of their charges and also information supplied by the children themselves in response to standard psychological tests. And fairly uniform conclusions have been reached indicating that probably only relatively small numbers of children and young people have suffered serious psychological damage, serious enough that is to warrant referral to specialist psychiatric services. Many others probably have also suffered but less severely and for much shorter periods of time. Contrary to expectations, however, the vast majority of children in Northern Ireland have not become psychological casualties of the troubles.

Several suggestions have been made as to why more children in Northern Ireland have not succumbed to the stresses of living with violence. One such suggestion is that the reaction of the child's family, particularly the parents, has played an important role. Also the child's own coping processes have been implicated and in this area two major hypotheses have been considered: the first is that children have simply become used to violence and the threat of violence; the second is that children (and adults) have learned to cope with the violence by either denying its existence or, perhaps more likely, denying its severity. At present however not enough evidence is available to choose between these two possibilities and more research will therefore be required to illuminate this important problem.

4

Moral Development

As the preceding chapters have demonstrated, children in Northern Ireland have for the last fifteen years been growing up in the midst of a society in turmoil. A society in which they have before them the example of adults unable to settle arguments except by stone throwing and/or murder and in which the forces of law and order have been openly challenged. Indeed, not only have children been mere observers but some at least have also been active participants in these activities. Small wonder therefore that before the troubles had been going for very long a veritable clamour of voices began to express anxiety about the moral development of Northern Ireland's young people forced to live in an apparently amoral society.

A Lost Generation?

These anxieties took two basic forms. First there was the fear that the anti-authority attitudes prevalent in a political context in Northern Ireland would generalise to other areas of society. As early as the early 1970s some observers claimed to be able to see this process at work. For example, in 1973 Fraser, the Belfast based child psychiatrist, was speaking of the ease with which anti-authority attitudes were generalising and noted that this was 'evident in all major sectors' of the children's lives (Fraser, 1974, 158). Similarly Fields (1973), as a result of her safaris from America to Northern Ireland, predicted '. . . the truncation of the development of moral judgement in a whole generation of children. . .'. While the cynical might accuse some of these authors of sensationalism in order to promote book sales the same could hardly be said of the Report of the Working Party from the Irish Council of Churches/Roman Catholic Church Joint Group on Social Questions. Yet they too noted, in that part of their report entitled 'Violence in Ireland', that:

With the general disorder consequent upon the use of violence has gone a serious deterioration in moral standards. There has been a catastrophic and terrifying decline in respect for the sacredness of human life. Consciences have become callous in respect of murder, torture, maiming; and needless to say also of destruction of property and injuries to persons. (Violence in Ireland, 1976, 48)

And not only had minds been numbed to the horrors around them, according to the report the cancer had spread further. The result was, they claimed, an increase in vandalism and theft, a 'disastrous' increase in excessive drinking and 'disturbing' signs of a breakdown in standards of sexual morality.

The second major concern for Northern Ireland watchers at this time (the early 1970s) was that as the Violence in Ireland report puts it 'it may take generations before the terrible moral and spiritual price for these years of violence is paid.' In other words a widespread fear was, and indeed still is, that when peace returns to Northern Ireland 'acts of violence and anti-social behaviour will continue because of the conditioning of previous years' (Lyons, 1973, 37).

Unfortunately at the time of writing this latter hypothesis cannot yet be tested – peace has still not broken out in Northern Ireland. But the earlier predictions of a general decline in moral standards, decreasing respect for authority and increased criminality among the young can now be examined using evidence from many different sources accumulated over the last fifteen years.

Religious Attitudes and Behaviour

Not unnaturally, the report to the churches had expressed concern not only for the moral development of children in Northern Ireland but for their spiritual development also. Certainly in the pre-troubles era in Northern Ireland the two had gone hand in hand in what was avowedly a uniquely Christian society. The churches, of all hues, had been the guardians of the people's moral standards. Now it appeared that the challenge to their moral teaching was a direct challenge to their general standing in the community.

Before the troubles began observers had been struck by the apparent religiosity of the people of Northern Ireland (Barritt and Carter, 1962). For as Rose (1976) has noted if religiosity is to be measured by church attendance then 'Northern Ireland is probably the most Christian society in the western world except for the Republic of Ireland.' An obvious question then is, has the hold of the churches over the people of Northern Ireland declined as a result of the conflict, as many had feared it might. More particularly, what influence does the church now have with a generation of young people who have known little else other than a background to their lives which has been decidedly unchristian?

Fortunately two studies have been conducted in this area, both concerned with young people and religion and both uniquely able to compare data gathered before the troubles began with data gathered ten years later when the violence was in full swing. In the first of these studies John Greer asked almost 2,000 boys and girls in their final year of secondary school (usual age eighteen to nineteen years) questions about their religious practices and beliefs. The survey was carried out in predominantly Protestant schools in various parts of Northern Ireland in 1968 and repeated in 1978. In his 1968 survey on adults, Rose (1972) had found that about 66 per cent of Protestants attended church monthly or more often. In the same year Greer's figures reveal a similar pattern for older adolescents with 65 per cent of boys and 76 per cent of girls attending church at least monthly. Ten years later, after ten years of the worst violence Northern Ireland has ever seen the figures revealed only a slight drop in church attendance with 56 per cent of boys and 68 per cent of girls now reporting that they were regular church attenders. This was the general pattern of results for other religious practices such as praying and Bible reading. In both 1968 and 1978 more girls than boys reported that they prayed daily or read the Bible but over the ten-year period virtually no changes occurred in the percentages of young people engaging in these particular practices. And a similar sort of pattern emerged when the questions measured religious beliefs. For example, some 60 per cent of boys in 1968 either were 'completely confident' or 'fairly sure' that God exists while the corresponding figure for 1978 was 61 per cent. Similarly, 78 per cent of girls in 1968 believed in God's existence while 73 per cent did so in 1978.

Greer (1980) a clergyman and religious educator, perhaps not surprisingly tended to emphasise the negative aspects of these results writing of 'the slow decline of traditional religious practice' as revealed in his study, which he felt stood in marked contrast to the relatively constant level of religious beliefs revealed in the survey. Nevertheless the results are, at least to the naive observer, remarkable for their lack of change over a decade which had witnessed otherwise enormous changes in Northern Irish society.

Further, it would appear that some confidence can be placed in these results because they have been replicated, to a certain extent, in a study by Turner *et al.* (1980). The Turner study was this time confined to boys, and only boys living in the Belfast area, but again was repeated over a ten-year period, this time in 1969 and 1979. In each year of the study some 800 boys representing four age levels – twelve, thirteen, fourteen, and fifteen years – drawn from both Catholic and Protestant secondary schools, answered questions designed to measure attitudes towards religion. For example, the questionnaire included such items as 'God knows all my thoughts and movements', and 'there is no life after death.' Each item was answered using a Likert type scale – 'strongly agree', 'agree', 'uncertain', 'disagree' and 'strongly disagree'. Altogether there were twenty-five such items and the total score on the questionnaire could range from zero to one hundred.

In the event the boys at each age level, in both years, always scored greater than 50, which Turner and his colleagues suggest may be taken to represent a 'neutral' score. In other words, on average regardless of age or the year in which they were tested these Belfast boys indicated that they possessed a generally positive attitude towards religion. Thus in 1969 the average score was 70.41 and in 1979 it was 68.52. However, these two figures actually conceal some interesting differences. To begin with Catholic boys tended to score at a somewhat higher level but tended to show a slight decrease from 1969 (77.21) to 1979 (73.29). The scores for Protestant boys on the other hand remained virtually stationary over the ten years at 63.61 in 1969 and 63.75 in 1979. Also age differences emerged in both years suggesting a general decline in religious attitudes with age from a maximum score at the twelve-year level to a minimum at the fifteen-year level.

It is of course possible to argue, as Turner *et al.* (1980) do, that 'in terms of deeply rooted social and personal values, a decade may be regarded as a very short time.' Nevertheless, given the fact that both the study by Turner *et al.* and that by Greer span not just any decade in any country but the first ten years of the troubles in Northern Ireland, the results of both studies are notable for the stability of religious attitudes, beliefs and practices that they reveal. Given that this particular decade was seen by some at least as one in which progressive secularisation might have been expected to occur anyway, troubles or no troubles, thus bringing Northern Irish young people into line with the rest of the western world, the results are all the more remarkable.

Indeed, it could perhaps be argued that the conflict in Northern

Ireland with its focus of identity firmly rooted in denominational membership, may have acted to artificially maintain religious loyalties. In this case, measures of religious attitudes and practices etc. may not be providing a particularly good guide to whether anti-authority attitudes have really been developing among young people in Northern Ireland as a result of their exposure to the political conflict and its attendant violence.

Moral Attitudes

A better approach therefore might be one which attempts to measure moral attitudes directly. This is exactly what John Greer did in his study of eighteen to nineteen-year-olds in Northern Ireland in 1968 and 1978. All the young people in his study, as well as being asked about their religious beliefs and practices were asked to respond on a four point scale from 'always wrong' to 'never wrong' to a series of moral issues. These included such things as gambling, suicide, war etc. What Greer (1980) found was that, comparing the proportion who endorsed 'always wrong' in 1968 with those who did so in 1978, relatively few changes had occurred over the ten year period. However, those few changes that were large enough to be considered statistically significant were in response to the items 'pre-marital sexual intercourse', 'capital punishment' and 'smoking'. Here attitudes towards the latter had become stricter for both boys and girls while greater permissiveness (i.e. fewer saying 'always wrong') characterised both boys' and girls' responses to the former two categories. Again what is surprising here is that given the length of the time interval, ten years, and the fact that these ten years embraced the start of the troubles in Northern Ireland, more changes did not occur. Greer's results also provide a valuable insight into the moral attitudes of Northern Irish young people compared to a similar group in England. This is because most of the questions Greer used had been included in a similar survey carried out by Wright and Cox in 1970 which involved some 1,500 school pupils aged between seventeen and nineteen years (Wright and Cox, 1971). What comparisons between the 1968 Northern Irish results and the 1970 English results reveal is that to almost every item more Northern Irish young people endorsed the 'always wrong' category. The most notable example of this is in the area of sexual morality where 26 per cent of the Northern Irish boys but only 10.3 per cent of the English boys thought 'pre-marital sexual intercourse' was 'always wrong' with the difference between girls even more marked at 51.2 per cent (Northern Irish) and 14.6 per cent (English). Indeed, of the eight items common to both surveys only one – smoking – produced comparable figures for both countries with 17.4 per cent and 20.9 per cent of boys and 19.7 per cent and 18.2 per cent of girls in Northern Ireland and England respectively judging smoking to be 'always wrong'.

Greer's results are thus most informative suggesting not only that little change in attitudes to moral issues occurred over the period 1968-78 but also that Northern Irish young people who are still at school in the eighteen to nineteen year age groups take a more rigid approach to these issues than do a similar group of English young people. Indeed, while the comparisons noted above involved 1968 for the Northern Irish sample and 1970 for the English survey, because these two time periods are relatively close together it is interesting to note that comparing the 1978 Northern Irish results with the 1970 English results still leaves the Northern Irish respondents ahead on moral rectitude. Of course, it is important to note, as Wright and Cox (1971) do, that just because something is not judged 'always wrong' it does not necessarily mean that it is therefore judged as 'never wrong'. Instead, they suggest, what their results indicate is that English young people in 1970 reveal 'an awareness of the complexity of moral problems and a disinclination to adopt extreme and uncompromising positions.' This, as we shall see, is a particularly illuminating remark, suggesting as it does the corollary that Northern Irish young people are not so aware of the complexity of moral problems.

The approach adopted by Greer (1980) and by Wright and Cox (1971) has a certain appeal. Young people are asked to judge pertinent moral issues in a straightforward way. Unfortunately the approach is limited. To begin with it is limited in that it is likely to be of little use in working with younger children. Secondly, it is limited in that the issues at stake are likely to be somewhat culture specific and therefore comparisons across cultures become difficult. Indeed, in the present context it is interesting to note that Greer, working in Northern Ireland, included as items on his questionnaire 'war' and 'capital punishment' and while these were not included in the English survey, that survey did ask about both 'non-addictive drugs' and 'addictive drugs' both of which were absent from the Irish version.

An alternative approach is to attempt to measure moral reasoning as opposed to moral attitudes, the idea being that moral reasoning is to some extent content free. This is a research area in which psychologists in many parts of the world have been active for some years, inspired by the ideas of the emminent child psychologist Jean Piaget. Piaget's pioneering work in this area has been developed largely as a result of the efforts of an American psychologist Lawrence Kholberg, whose major contribution has been to provide ways of measuring moral development during childhood. In general this work has indicated that as children get older they pass through three overlapping stages of moral development. In the first or Preconventional Stage children tend to adopt a concrete individual perspective on morality. In the second or Conventional Stage they adopt what is usually referred to as a 'member of society' perspective and in the third and final Principled Stage children come to believe in the validity of universal moral principles.

Working with a colleague called Tapp (Tapp and Kholberg, 1971), Kholberg demonstrated that orientation to the general issues of law and justice was influenced by the stages of moral development identified earlier by Kholberg. In their original study children were interviewed and asked a number of questions such as 'What would happen if there were no rules?', 'Why should people follow rules?', 'Can rules be changed?' or 'Are there times when it might be right to break a rule?' The results of this study illustrated that as children got older the reasons for obeying laws developed from simple avoidance of punishment through social conformity to ideas about laws as having beneficial and/or rational purposes. Similarly on the question of ever breaking a rule, younger children presented unqualified adherence to rules while at the other end of the age range university students tended to hold the view that moral considerations can take precedent even over legal considerations.

Surprisingly very few investigators have adopted Kholberg's approach to measuring moral development in research in Northern Ireland. The best known example of this approach appears in the work of the American psychologist Rona Fields who during a series of visits to Northern Ireland administered the Tapp and Kholberg questions (outlined above) to a number of children in various parts of Ireland (Fields, 1973; Fields, 1975). In the most recent account of this work (Fields, 1975) she compares the answers of children from Belfast at two different time periods 1971-2 and 1973-4 with those of children from Dublin (the capital of the Republic of Ireland) and from America. This latter American sample were in fact the children tested by Tapp and Kholberg as part of their original study. For the purposes of these comparisons the children were divided into either primary school children (age six to ten years) or middle school children (eleven to fourteen years).

And what these results appear to suggest is that at both age levels the children from Dublin and the USA showed similar patterns of moral reasoning about legal issues while the Belfast children were behind in their development in this context. For example, when asked 'Can rules be changed?' some 60 per cent of the Dublin children and 70 per cent of the American younger age children replied 'yes'. In comparison only 2 per cent of the Belfast children in 1971-2 and none of the Belfast children in 1973-4 responded in this way. Similarly, at the older age level 54 per cent of the Dublin children and 60 per cent of the children in the USA replied 'yes' to the question about rule changing but only 36 per cent and 30 per cent of the Belfast children did so in 1971-2 and 1973-4 respectively. In the same fashion, when asked if there are times when it might be right to break a rule the older children in both Dublin (60 per cent) and the USA (73 per cent) mentioned, in the main, the morality of the prevailing circumstances or talked about the morality of rules (Dublin – 10 per cent /USA – 17 per cent). However, only 25 per cent of the Belfast children in 1971-2 and 10 per cent in 1973-4 mentioned the morality of the circumstances while in 1972-3 some 30 per cent mentioned the morality of rules but none did so in the following year (1973-4).

The message coming from the results is therefore, according to Fields, very clear and it is that children from Belfast, at least in the early 1970s, were retarded in their moral development. And this is not just simply an Irish phenomenon because Irish children in Dublin did not show this lag in development. Rather it would appear to be a consequence of actually growing up in Belfast and hence, one might be justified in concluding, of growing up in a period of violence and unrest. Further, the evidence that Fields provides suggests that, if anything, this moral retardation may be getting worse as the length of time that children are exposed to a society in turmoil increases.

Unfortunately, although the conclusions are clear, just how one should evaluate the evidence on which the conclusions are based is more problematic. To begin with, as Fields (1973) herself points out, it is questionable whether her own results could be properly compared with the American sample gathered by Tapp and Kholberg. This is because the American sample was drawn on a random basis unlike either of the Irish samples. Indeed, her Belfast sample was confined to children of working-class parents and was recruited solely on the basis of personal contact. Further, the size of the US sample was much greater than either the Dublin (22) or the Belfast samples (78) totalled over both years. As Fields (1973) concludes 'the two sample populations [sic] cannot therefore be legitimately compared for statistical significance for these reasons.' Nevertheless she then goes on to do just that and to make such comparisons.

Even if one were to accept Field's results at face value a puzzling aspect of the whole thing is how children who had been exposed to Northern Irish society as we know it today for only three to four years at the most, could be so retarded in an area of their development which had undoubtedly been underway long before the troubles began. The answer according to Fields is that Northern Irish society as a whole is and (more important in this context) was, morally retarded, and that this retardation existed and influenced its children well before the current troubles actually began. Therefore, according to her the developmental process for these children occurred in a milieu of authoritarianism and hierarchical ordering with no prospect of political efficacy for them any more than there had been for their parents. Thus, says Fields, the moral reasoning of the children and young people, particularly with respect to the topic of law and order had been 'truncated' because the authoritarian regime in which they had grown up always carried with it the implication that power was the property of the strongest.

Certainly these conclusions, despite the fact that they are based on rather flimsy evidence, seem to fit in with Greer's results where a comparison between English and Northern Irish children was possible. However, some important questions remain unanswered. Is this moral truncation which Fields spoke of a result of living in a society in the midst of political upheaval (both her results and Greer's results suggest not), is it simply a property of growing up in Northern Ireland or indeed is it simply an Irish phenomenon? One way to try to tease out the answers to these questions is to compare children who have grown up with the troubles with their peers in the Republic of Ireland and also, within Northern Ireland, to compare children from areas which have experienced greater or lesser levels of political violence. This is exactly what Breslin (1982) did in her study which compared over 1,000 seventeen-year-olds, Catholics and Protestants, attending schools in various parts of the Republic of Ireland and of Northern Ireland. Her measure of moral reasoning consisted of four moral dilemmas each centring around the issue of civil rights for a minority group *vis*. Communists, Jews, Blacks or Atheists. Each dilemma was followed by ten reasons for either granting or withholding civil rights to the group in question and the students were required to rank order these items in order of preference. The responses were then used to classify the respondents as being at either the advanced 'principled' stage of moral development (28 per cent) where the individual has the ability to apply moral standards in an autonomous and rational way, or at the less advanced 'conventional' stage (72 per cent) where the individual adopts the norms of his/her society largely without question.

Her most important findings were that while there were no differences between young people resident in the Republic and in Northern Ireland on the moral reasoning measure, Catholics did show a small but statistically significant superiority to Protestants regardless of area of residence. However, the most surprising result was that when the young people from Northern Ireland were classified according to whether they came from a region which had experienced 'high', 'medium' or 'low' levels of violence, the sample from the high violence area produced the highest mean moral reasoning score. Puzzled by this unexpected result Breslin (1982) went on to suggest that this might be because high levels of violence were confounded with high levels of urbanisation. That is the most violent areas were those which were most urbanised and this might therefore account for the high violence area's superiority in moral reasoning. However, what she failed to check apparently was the religious make-up of the samples from the high, medium and low violence areas. As there is a tendency for more violence to occur in predominantly Catholic areas (Poole, 1983), and as Breslin had already indicated a superiority for Catholics in the moral reasoning measure she employed, this could also explain these puzzling results. That is, it may simply have been that Catholics were over-represented in the sample from the high violence area.

However one interprets that particular finding Breslin's work is certainly important in that it suggests no difference in moral reasoning between a Northern Irish sample of young people and a sample from the Republic. Further, and perhaps most importantly, it provides no evidence that within Northern Ireland itself exposure to higher levels of violence has retarded moral development. Unfortunately, a major weakness in Breslin's (1982) study is that the measure of moral development employed was not one that had been used by other investigators in other parts of the world. Therefore, her study casts no light on the possibility that it is Irish children in general who are morally retarded in comparison to English or American children as hinted at in the results obtained by Greer (1980) and Fields (1973) respectively.

Fortunately two other studies do provide further evidence on this topic. In a small scale but tightly designed study Cairns and Conlin (1985) compared fifty-four girls from one of the parts of west Belfast worst affected by the violence with a group of thirty-four girls from Dublin. The study though small scale had the advantage that the two samples from Belfast and Dublin were alike in every possible respect except for their area of residence. This is because the girls, all aged fifteen years, were from predominantly working-class backgrounds, living in an inner city area, Catholic and attending Catholic secondary schools run by the same religious order in Belfast and Dublin respectively. Each of the girls was asked to complete a recently developed pencil and paper version of Kohlberg's moral reasoning interview (an individual interview task). This group test, the Sociomoral Reflection Objective Measure (SROM) requires each respondant to read two short stories which pose a moral dilemma and then to answer sixteen questions as to how these dilemmas might be resolved (Gibbs *et al.*, 1984). For example, the first dilemma concerns a man whose wife is dying of cancer. The man, we are told, cannot afford to buy the drug necessary to save his wife's life. Should he break the law and steal the drug? The questions following then ask such things as why should he try to get the drug for his wife and what if the person dying is not the man's wife but just a friend, or indeed a stranger – does it make a difference and so on. All the answers are provided in multiple choice format.

What the results of this study indicated (Cairns and Conlin, 1985) was that whether one compared overall scores on the questionnaire, which could range from a minimum of 100 to a maximum of 500, or whether these scores were translated into stages of moral development *à la* Kohlberg, no significant differences were revealed between the Belfast and the Dublin samples. But once again when the scores of the Irish children (north or south) were compared with those from an American sample the results suggested that the Irish children (mean score 273.67) were slightly behind their North American peers (mean score 323.75 for a group of fourteen-year-olds and 354.95 for a group of sixteen-year-olds). And these conclusions are in broad agreement with those reached by Kahn (1982) who, using a different measure of moral reasoning, the Defining Issues Test, with children in the Republic of Ireland only, also found that the average score for his Irish sample was lower than the accepted American norms for similar aged children. Also, of course, the Cairns and Conlin (1985) study confirms the finding of Breslin, and the trend implicit in the results of Greer's study, that growing up in the midst of a society in a state of political upheaval and constantly learning of murder and maiming being used by adults to settle their quarrels has surprisingly not had any detrimental influence on the moral reasoning of Northern Irish children.

It could be argued that these studies are not a direct test of the fears that have been expressed concerning the moral development of children in Northern Ireland. This is because one of the most prominent concerns with adults has been that children in Northern Ireland, exposed to so much aggression on the part of adults in their society, will learn that the only way to resolve conflicts is through the use of violence. In other words, the worry has perhaps not been so much that their general moral reasoning will have been affected but rather that in this one specific area they will have adopted the moral standards of the warring tribes in Northern Ireland.

To date only one study has tested this idea directly – that of Cairns (1983a). To examine children's ideas about the morality of violence used to settle personal conflict Cairns made use of a technique, adapted from Thomas and Drabmann (1977), which measures the level of violence children feel is justified in a series of situations typical of those they might find themselves in at school or with their friends. The test consists of a series of such situations which are described to the children, followed by a set of possible responses to that situation. For example, 'A boy is playing a game and keeps making mistakes, another boy starts making fun of him. Should the first boy. . . ?' The possible responses represent either 'physical aggression', 'verbal aggression', 'leaving the field' or 'positive coping'. The responses are presented in the form of two pairs of stick figures, each pair illustrating, and labelled with, one of the possible responses. For example, the child might be presented with a pair of stick figures which would be labelled 'throw something at the other boy' (i.e. physical aggression) or a pair labelled 'go some-where else'(i.e. leaving the field). In each pair a boy (stick figure) would be seen either throwing something or walking away. Each situation was followed by all possible paired combinations of the four alternative responses making a total of six choices about how to respond in each situation. For any one situation the score could range from a minimum of 1, which meant that an aggressive response (physical or verbal) was chosen only when two aggressive responses were pitted against one another to a maximum of 5 which meant an aggressive response was chosen every time one was presented. Overall a child's score for the whole test was the sum of the scores across the nine situations described meaning that total scores could range from a low of 9 to a high of 45.

The whole test was presented twice to some 600 children (Cairns, 1983a). On the first administration the children were asked to respond in the way they thought *most* boys of their age would behave in these situations. On the second administration the instructions were altered and the children were asked to choose the response they thought was the 'right thing' or 'very best thing' to do. The results suggested that to begin with children realise that how most boys behave in such situations is very different from the way they ought to behave. Thus mean aggressiveness scores (verbal plus physical) on the 'normative' version of the test were 33.84 compared to 14.51 on the 'morality' version. In other words, most boys are seen to behave much more aggressively in interpersonal conflict situations in comparison to the level of aggression required if they were doing the 'right thing'. Further, while girls and boys were agreed about how most boys actually behave, girls chose fewer aggressive responses as the 'right thing' compared to boys. But what is of particular interest here is that whether the children involved lived in an area of the Republic of Ireland (where there has been no political violence) or in areas of Northern Ireland which have suffered either low or high levels of violence (objectively determined) they were agreed as to what was the right level of violence to use in the situations described to them. In other words, exposure to real life violence did not seem to alter their ideas about the morality of violence. Of course, it should be made clear that the test employed by Cairns (1983a) measured only aggression in interpersonal situations. This study therefore does not indicate whether, when these children grow up they will or will not approve of the use of violence for political ends. It does however provide some evidence to challenge those pessimists who have suggested that Northern Ireland's political or intergroup violence may be spilling over into interpersonal situations.

Morality and Behaviour: School Attendance

Moral reasoning measures are of course essentially measures of optimum performance – the best that children can do if they really try. But there is no guarantee that this is the level they will actually operate at in the real world. Moral behaviour undoubtedly depends on other factors, including such things as the particular situation and peer pressure. For reasons such as these not everyone is going to be entirely convinced by the results of paper and pencil measures completed by random samples of children and young people. After all, it can be argued, these studies simply reflect, at best, children's attitudes towards moral issues or, even more obscurely, their ability to reason in moral terms. What the results of these surveys do not give is any indication of the children's actual behaviour. Therefore, it is as well, at this point, to examine the evidence available concerning how children in Northern Ireland are actually behaving – morally or otherwise.

An obvious place to look for evidence of amoral behaviour in its widest sense is the school setting. Here surely any signs that children were rebelling against the established order would make itself felt – and quickly. Strangely, little formal research seems to have been carried out in this area. Virtually the only evidence available which provides an insight into children's behaviour towards their teachers comes from McKeown's (1973) survey of secondary school headmasters (*see* Chapter 3 for further details). This disclosed that in response to the question 'Has there been a growing lack of respect for the authority of the class teacher over the past three years?', the 150 schools which answered this question were evenly divided into those who said 'yes' and those who said 'no'. A more detailed breakdown suggests that Catholic schools were more likely to answer in the affirmative, as were a separate group of schools which were located in an area where serious disturbances had occurred. Further, this report also records that approximately one third of all schools indicated that there had been an increase in vandalism during the school day and over half reported an increase in vandalism after school hours. Also a majority of schools reported an increase in the use of 'foul' language by their pupils. What the survey could not say, however, as McKeown (1974) notes, is how far these changes are the consequences of the civil disturbances and how far they are simply due to social changes influencing all of Western society.

One possible reason why more schools did not report a 'growing lack of respect for authority' may have been that this lack of respect for authority was not in evidence in the classroom because the children most likely to behave in this way were not there either. Certainly in the early 1970s rumours were rife that 'mitching' as it is colloquially known, or being absent from school without permission, had reached epidemic proportions. For example, Fraser (1974) claimed, without producing detailed facts to back up his assertion, that attendance was down to 70 per cent in most schools in troubled areas and sometimes to 50 per cent or less. This however contrasts markedly with the impressions of school headmasters as recorded in the Secondary Schools Survey conducted by McKeown (1973). When asked 'How has your attendance been affected by civil unrest?' some 52 per cent replied 'not at all', 40 per cent 'to some extent' and only 6 per cent replied 'to a large extent'. Of course, there were schools situated in all parts of Northern Ireland. However, even the results from the schools in areas which, on their own admission, had seen serious disturbances, reflected a similar lack of concern with only some 27 per cent reporting their attendance levels had been affected 'to a large extent' by the troubles.

This is of course a rather subjective measure of absenteeism. How headmasters decided whether their school had suffered to a 'large extent' or not obviously may have varied from school to school, depending on many factors including the pre-troubles level of attendance. Fortunately more objective information has since become available in the form of the report of two surveys from the Department of Education in Northern Ireland, concerned with persistent school absenteeism in 1977 and 1982. This is not to imply that no information was available from official sources before that date. For example, it was known that in the Belfast area, over the period 1968 to 1977, primary schools (roughly five to ten years) had been showing a fairly steady state of attendance with minor fluctuations around the 91 per cent mark. Secondary schools (eleven to sixteen plus years) had however shown a steady drop at least until 1974 but then had levelled off at around 84 per cent (*Persistent School Absenteeism*, 1977). However, as the first Department of Education report points out, the figures only present a very gross and hence misleading picture. In particular what such data do not make clear is how many children were absent for a genuine reason, especially physical illness, and how many were absent for other less acceptable reasons. To obtain more information on these latter 'unjustified' absences a survey was carried out in the spring term of 1977. Because the primary focus was *persistent* absenteeism detailed information was only recorded for children who had been absent on more than fourteen days in that particular term. Using this strict criterion, only 7.8 per cent of the compulsory school age population of Northern Ireland were considered to be persistent absentees. This 7.8 per cent, which consisted of roughly equal numbers of boys and girls, contained within it some 14,000 children (or 4.2 per cent of the school population) who were absent for reasons other than physical illness.

Examining these cases in more detail revealed that now boys were slightly over-represented (54.5 per cent) and also that while only 1.8 per cent of the five to ten years age group were unjustifiably absent 11.6 per cent of the fifteen to sixteen years age group were included in this category. This, it should be noted, was in marked contrast to the breakdown by age of those who were absent for reasons of physical illness where the children were roughly equally spread across the three age bands five to ten years, eleven to fourteen years and fifteen to sixteen years.

The report also examined the absenteeism levels for the five education boards in Northern Ireland. In this respect the Belfast area had the worst record at most ages and for both sexes. The one exception to this was fifteen to sixteen-year-old boys in the Western Board who led the league table in their age group. As Harbison and Caven (1980) note in a paper analysing further some of the data in the original report, Londonderry schools with their high rates were what almost certainly raised the absenteeism rates in the Western area. These figures are of particular interest because Belfast and Derry were the cities which had witnessed the greatest political upheaval during the 1970s. Of course, not all of Belfast suffered the consequences of violence to the same extent and here it is interesting that the report was able to demonstrate that even within the Belfast area absenteeism rates were not uniform across schools. Rather there appeared to be pockets of particularly high absenteeism vividly illustrated by the fact that the report was able to identify seven schools with pupils in the age range eleven to fourteen years which contained about 48 per cent of the persistent non-attenders in the Belfast area but only 18 per cent of the area's children in that age range. These data take on even greater significance because the writers of the government report were able to compare the Belfast figures with those of a similar English city – Sheffield. This revealed that the figures for absenteeism in Belfast in 1977 were just a little higher than those in the five to ten years group in Sheffield in 1974 but significantly higher in the eleven to fourteen years group and the fifteen to sixteen years group. Indeed, in this latter category the report notes the problem in Belfast was two and a half times as great as in Sheffield.

All this appears to paint a rather black picture with unjustified absences running at a high level especially in certain Belfast schools. Indeed, this would seem to confirm that Belfast's children or at least some of them, in certain parts of the city, had in the lawless climate of the early seventies got badly out of control. Out of control to the extent that they were no longer attending school regularly even though they were fit to do so. The puzzling fact however is that this description really only appears to fit a small minority of the persistently absent (12 per cent), for the vast majority (57 per cent) of the unjustifiable absentees were in fact absent with their parents' consent. It would appear therefore that, far from casting aside society and its rules, the children of Belfast, even in the violent days of 1977, were largely still under control – even if not attending school. One can of course only speculate as to why so many parents kept or allowed children to remain at home rather than go to school and the obvious answer (Heskin, 1980) is because parents feared for the safety of the children either on the journey to school or indeed in school itself. Certainly in the 1970s attacks on children on their way to school by rival factions were not unknown and some schools even became targets for bombers and gunmen. After all 1977 – although by Northern Irish standards not a particularly violent year (112 deaths) – was just one year after the province had experienced four very violent years in which, on average, 250 deaths per year had occurred. It may be, therefore, that parents still felt anxious about the safety of their children even though in reality the level of violence had dropped dramatically.

If this explanation is correct then a similar survey carried out at a later time, with a similar level of violence should show a decrease in levels of absenteeism. And this is exactly what the next Department of Education survey did show. Designed to replicate the 1977 survey in every way, the good news was that in 1982 in both absolute and relative terms, there was a big reduction in the number of children absent for reasons other than physical illness – a drop from 4.2 per cent of the total school population in 1977 to 2 per cent in 1982. But inexplicably, in a year with 'only' 97 deaths, condoned absences, that is those with parental approval, had now risen to account for 68.4 per cent of the total not due to physical illness. Where the biggest drop had occurred from 1972 to 1982 was in the enigmatic category 'absent with parent's knowledge but unable to insist on return', a decrease from 20.8 per cent to 12 per cent of all non-physical illness absences.

How one interprets these data is open to argument. Certainly they appear to contradict the earlier prophets of doom who had argued that once children in Northern Ireland had established the habit of defying authority, as many apparently did in the early 1970s, then they would be a generation for ever lost to adult control. Worse, the next generation, seeing their older brothers and sisters flaunting authority, would follow suit and so the pattern would be established unbroken for generations to come. The figures on absenteeism most definitely refute this latter assertion. Not only had attendance figures improved from 1977 to 1982 but where absenteeism continued to exist, it remained a characteristic of older children (fifteen to sixteen years) and showed no signs of spreading its influence among their younger brothers and sisters.

That is of course the good news. The bad news, pessimists could point out, is that tucked away amidst the welter of statistics in the second Department of Education Report on Persistent School Absenteeism (1982) is the statement 'children traditionally described as "truanting", defined as being absent without parental knowledge or consent, accounted for 11 per cent of absences for reasons other than physical illness.' This statistic takes on particular significance for two reasons. First it means that the proportion of unjustified absences which could be described as truanting had shown virtually no decline from its 12 per cent level in 1977. (This is not to suggest of course that in absolute terms or indeed as a proportion of the total school population a reduction had not occurred.) The second reason that this statistic is important is because, as Heskin (1980) notes, a truancy problem is 'by implication' a delinquency problem, because truancy cases are liable to end up as court cases. Further, there is always the suspicion that it is this group of children, those who can be considered as true truants, who are most likely during their time away from school to run foul of the law.

Morality and Behaviour: Juvenile Crime

What then of the statistics on juvenile crime – that is, juvenile crime excluding 'political' crime dealt with in Chapter 1. What picture do they paint of the way children and young people have been behaving in Northern Ireland? Is it true as reported by the Churches Report on Violence in Ireland that 'a concomitant of political violence has been a great increase in plain vandalism, theft and crime'? Or was this simply a view held by a group of otherworldly clergymen out of touch with life on the streets? According to Caul (1983) and McCauley and Cunningham (1983), papers prepared for circulation within government departments at that time (the early 1970s) also anticipated the likelihood of an 'imminent and dramatic increase in juvenile delinquency' (McCauley and Cunningham, 1983, 84). This increase was apparently predicted by government experts both because of the deteriorating economic situation in Northern Ireland and the predicted prolonged effects on young people of continuing exposure to the civil conflict. Indeed, according to Caul (1983) something resembling 'moral panic' had gripped the Northern Irish establishment during this period and was particularly influential in its thinking about juvenile crime. Indeed, the expectation was, in government circles, that the increase in juvenile delinquency would be such as to swamp the existing specialist services in this area.

These gloomy predictions on the part of civil servants are all the more surprising given that the official statistics for the period 1968-72 had actually revealed a dramatic decrease in the number of crimes committed by young people. Considering that this period coincided with the time when the civil disturbances in Northern Ireland were involving more people – adults and children – than at any other time in lawlessness, largely in the form of street rioting, this is a remarkable outcome. Paradoxically it may have been this decreasing trend which led government experts to predict an overall increase in juvenile crime in the coming years. This is because this decrease in the 1968-72 period was interpreted as being due to the preoccupation of the police with other priorities in Northern Ireland at this time. This interpretation receives some support from the fact that detection rates for offences known to the police also fell dramatically during this period, from 58 per cent in 1968 to 21 per cent in 1972 (Caul, 1983).

Indeed, the phenomenon of low detection rates on the part of the police has continued into the 1980s (PPRU Occasional Paper No.5, 1984) and may in turn be related to the fact that although juvenile crime increased from its low in 1972 it has remained fairly constant over the period 1975 onwards, when it again attained its 1970 level (Caul, 1983). Curran (1984) suggests that these two phenomena are related, that is low police detection rates and non-rising juvenile crime, and takes this to indicate that in Northern Ireland there must exist a substantial proportion of hidden or 'dark crime' offences which are either unknown to the police or do not find their way into official statistics. Research in the USA and in England and Wales has certainly suggested that such crime does exist but little evidence for its existence in Northern Ireland has been obtained to date. A preliminary report of data contained in the Northern Ireland Continuous Household Survey does however suggest that indeed a discrepancy may exist between official rates of crime and actual rates of crime (PPRU, 1984) and that this discrepancy may be greatest where less serious crime is concerned. Indeed, it does not require much imagination to think of reasons why not all people in Northern Ireland would wish to report all crimes to the police. For example, certain sections of the community may simply reject the help of the police for political reasons. Others may feel that the police are either powerless or unwilling to act in certain cases. Yet others may fear retaliation if they involve the police. Also Caul (1983) suggests that the existence of an alternative justice system instigated in some areas by the paramilitary organisations, who have been known to hand out rough justice (for example knee-cappings) via their 'kangaroo courts', may have had an impact on the amount of crime reported to the police.

Despite this sort of evidence it remains difficult to estimate whether the amount of unreported crime in Northern Ireland is really any different to the amount of unreported crime in, for example, England and Wales. Heskin (1981) argues that it almost certainly is not less because, firstly, Northern Ireland is a small country and this limits the amount of crime that can go unnoticed by the police and, secondly, because of the high level of police and army intelligence gathering operations which presumably increase the amount of known crime. And if it is not, then one must take comfort from the fact that all the experts seem to be in agreement that the proportion of young people involved in crimes in Northern Ireland is substantially lower than that in England and Wales and that this has been a consistent trend for at least the last two decades (Caul, 1983; Curran, 1984). On the other hand, Caul (1983) reports that he suspects that a modest but steady increase in juvenile crime has begun to reveal itself since about 1978. The complexity of the issues involved here however is illustrated by the fact that Jardine (1983) feels more young people are being drawn into the criminal justice system because the police have increased the number of cautions issued to young people in recent years from 17 per cent in 1977 to 49 per cent in 1983. What this means is that while the police took action against 52 per cent more juveniles in 1981 than in 1977, 600 fewer were actually prosecuted and in excess of 2,000 *more* were cautioned (Jardine, 1983).

Another consideration which also complicates the way one must try to answer the question, 'Have the troubles led more young people in Northern Ireland to become involved in crime?' is the fact that in Northern Ireland, as elsewhere, young people do not stay young people for ever. This means, for instance, that the fifteen to sixteen-year-olds of the early seventies, if they took up a life of crime have swollen the adult crime statistics, not the juvenile crime statistics. Perhaps therefore it is to the adult crime statistics that we must look in order to decide if the moral standards of young people in Northern Ireland have been influenced by the political unrest of the last fifteen years.

Here, in contrast to the figures for crimes committed by juveniles, the total crime figures have shown a steady escalation from around ten crimes known to the police per 1,000 population in 1968 to thirty per thousand in 1978 and around forty-one in 1983. An immediate suspicion must of course be that this rise can be substantially accounted for by the increase in 'political' crime over this period, particularly murder and attempted murder. However, a recent government publication (PPRU, 1984) dispels this idea. What this report reveals is that at least from 1969 'violence against the person' has remained a virtual constant fraction of total crime known to the police, although within this category the number of murders and attempted murders increased sharply to a peak in 1972, but since has shown a general decrease. In fact what the statistics make clear is that theft and burglary account for the greatest proportion of crime in any particular year in Northern Ireland over the last fifteen to twenty years. Further, while, as a proportion of the total crime figures, theft and burglary have remained nearly constant, in absolute terms the amount of this type of crime has increased steadily in almost every year since the troubles began. Perhaps here at last is the evidence needed to confirm the long anticipated decline in moral standards in Northern Irish society. However, before leaping to such a conclusion two important facts must be taken into consideration. The first is that an increase in the level of crime in Northern Ireland was already underway before the troubles had begun. For example, in 1960 about six crimes per thousand were known to the police and this had grown to about thirteen in 1969. This would suggest that the increase in crime over the next two decades cannot be blamed solely on the troubles. However, even more convincing evidence that the increase in crime since the early 1970s must be largely attributable to something other than the troubles comes in a paper by Heskin (1981) which compares crime levels in Northern Ireland with those in the Republic of Ireland and in England and Wales over the period 1960-78 plus a similar comparison of crime levels in Belfast and Dublin over the period 1964-78. The outcome of this exercise is a clear demonstration that the rate of crime in Northern Ireland was always slightly higher than that in the Republic up until about 1969 when the troubles began. After this period however the gap between the two widened, reaching its maximum level in 1972. What is important, however, is that this trend did not continue and the gap between the two has thus remained virtually constant ever since, with roughly twice the number of crimes known to the police in Northern Ireland as in the Republic of Ireland. On the other hand crime in Northern Ireland, pre-troubles, was always at a lower level than that in England and Wales. However, as Heskin (1981) points out, between 1969 and 1972 this gap was seen to be narrowing in such a way that there was the distinct possibility that, if the trend continued, Northern Ireland might have actually over-taken Britain in terms of its crime rate. However, after 1972, because of the slow-down in the rate of increase in Northern Ireland, crime levels in Northern Ireland have continued to be lower than those in England and Wales. Nevertheless as Heskin (1981) notes, it could still be argued 'at the naive level' that the rate of indictable crime from 1960-78 has increased more in Northern Ireland than in either the Republic of Ireland or England and Wales. Heskin illustrates, however, that the rate of increase is dependent on the particular base rate chosen. For example, between 1960 and 1978 the increase was 507 per cent for Northern Ireland, 342 per cent for the Republic and 221 per cent for England and Wales. However, this same exercise based on the increase between 1972 and 1978 reveals increases of 130 per cent, 144 per cent, and 151 per cent for Northern Ireland, the Republic of Ireland and England and Wales respectively. The most remarkable feature of rates of crimes in these three areas is thus how closely they are related, which close relationship in turn makes it difficult to attribute the total increase in Northern Ireland's crime rate to a decline in moral standard resulting from the conflict. This conclusion is reinforced by a compari-son of crime levels in Dublin and Belfast. And this analysis Heskin (1981) claims is particularly damaging 'to the notion of a disintegrating society in Northern Ireland' because, as he rightly points out, if evidence of moral disintegration on a vast scale due to the troubles was to be found anywhere in Northern Ireland most surely it should be found in the city of Belfast.

Heskin's conclusion therefore is that 'the phenomena of civil conflict in Northern Ireland have pushed up the general level of crime beyond that which it might otherwise have been in the absence of the troubles. . . [but] . . . it is clear that the increase in crime due to the troubles has stabilised at quite a low level' (Heskin, 1981, 120). Indeed, a recent government publication on Northern Irish crime statistics (PPRU, 1984) goes rather further and tries to make the case that Northern

Ireland is a relatively law-abiding part of the world compared at least to similar sized and populated areas in either England and Wales or in the USA. Thus, for example, the report claims that the number of offences known to the police for every thousand people in Northern Ireland was, in 1981, 41.66, which is similar to Essex (41.31) or Staffordshire (41.94) in England or to Maine (41.38) or Nebraska (34.41) in the USA. Indeed, compared to seven areas of similar sized population in England and Wales and five in the US, Northern Ireland ranked tenth lowest in 1981 in terms of overall crime rates and certainly well behind the 87.05 crimes per thousand and 80.88 crimes per thousand in Merseyside and Northumbria respectively in England. Even when the overall crime rate is broken down into more specific crimes, Northern Ireland maintains its relatively low position. Only in two categories does Northern Ireland come near the top of this particular league table, and this is where murder and robbery are concerned. Northern Ireland is top of the table for robberies and second for murders with .07 murders per thousand (in 1981) compared to New Mexico with .10 and just ahead of Virginia with .068 but a long way ahead of any of the regions in England and Wales none of which tops the .018 mark.

These statistics therefore leave the reader a choice – either to rejoice that 'ordinary' crime in Northern Ireland is running at a fairly low level or to weep for its higher murder rate. Certainly if one accepts that the vast majority of the murders are at least politically inspired then one gets a picture of a rather schizophrenic society where strict moral ethics are still the order of the day – except of course where politics are concerned. However one interprets these data they do make the point that the immorality or amorality of political violence in Northern Ireland has apparently not generalised to other areas of behaviour and thus in one sense 'war-torn Ulster' is actually a relatively crime-free and moral society.

Conclusions

Despite the fears of educators, clergymen and others there appears to be little evidence that the moral standards of Northern Irish children have declined because of the political conflict and violence generated by the 'troubles'. Objective measures such as school absenteeism and juvenile crime rates do suggest that to begin with a slight increase in these behaviours may have accompanied the opening years of the violence but recent information suggests that the rate of acceleration has now settled down to that which is being experienced in other parts of the British Isles.

Indeed, thanks to the work of Greer we have evidence that young people's attitudes towards such moral issues as gambling, suicide etc. have remained relatively conservative over the first ten years of the troubles at least and almost certainly were more conservative than their English peers both before the conflict erupted and indeed since. The fact that young people in Northern Ireland, over a similar ten year period, showed a much greater tendency than young people in England to adopt uncompromising or extreme attitudes is particularly revealing, especially when taken together with the results of the studies which have attempted to measure not simply moral attitudes but the more subtle process of moral reasoning. What these studies suggest is that indeed the development of moral reasoning may be delayed in Northern Ireland – but only in comparison to children and young people in the USA. The moral truncation that Fields observed in Northern Ireland and attributed to the violence and political conflict now seems much more likely to be an Irish phenomenon rather than a conflict related phenomenon. Ireland is after all a rural, religious, conservative society and this description holds for both Northern Ireland and the Republic and regardless of whether Catholic or Protestant predominates.

The good news, therefore, is that this is a society where the majority of young people still at least have doubts about gambling, drunkenness and pre-marital sexual intercourse, where the majority attend school regularly, give relatively little trouble to their teachers, and largely keep on the right side of the law. This they do because they accept what their elders have told them – namely what is right and what is wrong. The bad news, however, is that it may be this same unquestioning attitude, this conservative outlook, which leads to a perpetuation of the 'Irish problem' from generation to generation. In turn this may mean that if one day the two communities are to live in 'peace and harmony' something will have to be done to ensure that Northern Ireland does not continue to produce generation after generation of unquestioning children and adults (a point taken up again in Chapter 7).

5

Taking Sides

The troubles, grim as they are, have been the source of a certain amount of humour, albeit at times rather black humour. What is interesting however is that often this humour provides revealing insights into the psychology of life in Northern Ireland. For example, in the present context with the focus on children in Northern Ireland the following is illuminating:

Two neighbours, one Protestant and the other Catholic, went to the seaside together. One had a small son, the other a daughter. Neither child had a swim suit but as the beach was remote the parents allowed them to paddle naked. Afterwards as the wee boy was being dried by his mother he remarked 'Mother, I never knew there was such a difference between Catholics and Protestants.'

This little story raises some important questions. For example, at what age do children in Northern Ireland become aware that in their society there is this fundamental cleavage of all life into Catholic and Protestant? Perhaps more importantly at what age do they learn that they belong to one or other of these two groups and how important this group membership is? These apparently simple questions, whose consideration will form the substance of this chapter, in turn lead to other more basic questions about the nature of the conflict itself and particularly the causes of the conflict. For example, one of the things that often puzzles those outside Northern Ireland is why the conflict has gone on for so long. Why is it that two sets of people living in Western Europe in the late twentieth century are apparently locked into a never-ending cycle of hatred whose roots can be traced back as far as the twelfth century? What exactly is in it for ordinary people that helps to keep the conflict alive? And what are the mechanisms involved?

Theoretical Explanations for Conflict

These are of course questions which have exercised the minds of social scientists over many years with reference to intergroup conflicts in general and not just that in Northern Ireland. Over the years two types of theory have been particularly popular with psychologists. The first of these suggests that intergroup conflicts are best explained in racial terms and are in some unknown way inherited and thus passed on from generation to generation. In other words, groups come into conflict, it is suggested, 'because it is a basic human instinct.' This type of theory is now known to be almost certainly incorrect. As we learn more and more about genetics it has become obvious that such molar behaviours as intergroup conflict are not the sort of messages carried by our genes. The second group of theories suggests that intergroup conflict is best viewed as some form of abnormal behaviour, perhaps a kind of group madness. Again this family of theories has received little support. Anyway, intergroup conflict cannot be properly considered as abnormal behaviour. To do so would be to dismiss half the world's population as mad, given that intergroup conflict is not confined to Northern Ireland, as news bulletins about the Lebanon, India, Cyprus, Srilanka, Brixton and Birmingham testify.

Both these ideas are attractive because they reduce a complex phenomenon to a few very simple ideas – ideas which fit well into newspaper headlines and political catchphrases. Even today one reads press reports about Northern Ireland which use words like tribal/barbaric or mindless/psychopathic. Fortunately, a recently developed socio-psychological theory (Tajfel, 1981) of intergroup conflict has now begun to influence thinking in this area. This theory will be used as a general background framework in this chapter in an attempt to understand better how children and young people in Northern Ireland come to take sides in the conflict, even perhaps to the extent where they are willing to die for their particular cause.

Tajfel's theory has several major advantages over all others (see Cairns, 1982, for a more detailed treatment of the theory applied to Northern Ireland) the most important being that it views intergroup conflict not as some form of irrational or abnormal behaviour but rather as behaviour which can be entirely explained in terms of normal psychological processes.

Put briefly what this theory suggests is that in every society a process called social categorisation is at work. This is used to make life simple, bearable indeed, by reducing the multiplicity of social stimuli we are faced with in everyday life to a smaller more manageable number of social categories. This has the effect of exaggerating differences between particular categories and also of minimising differences within categories. In other words, two people who are labelled as belonging to different social categories or groups are seen as rather more different than they actually are while two people from the same group are seen as rather less different than they actually are.

An important consequence of the process of social categorisation, according to Tajfel, is that we not only divide our social world into groups or categories but we inevitably see ourselves as belonging to certain of these social categories but not others. In other words, to use Tajfel's terms, we develop a social identity. These two processes – social categorisation and social identity – are, according to Tajfel (1978) very important links in the causal chain which underlines the development of intergroup conflict, because as Tajfel has pointed out:

> in order for large numbers of individuals to be able to hate or dislike or discriminate against other individuals seen as belonging to a common social category they must first have aquired a sense of belonging to groups (or social categories) which are clearly distinct from and stand in certain relations to, those they hate, dislike or discriminate against. (Tajfel, 1978, 50.)

According to Tajfel, this is not the total explanation for the development of intergroup conflict however. Rather he suggests that not only do we divide the world into social groups, and feel that we belong to certain of these social groups and thus develop a social identity, but we also wish to enhance our feeling about ourselves and one way of doing this is to ensure that our social identity is positively evaluated.

We do this by making comparisons between our own social group and others and ensuring that through these comparisons our group achieves 'social psychological distinctiveness'.

According to the theory, these processes are common in all human societies but do not necessarily lead to intergroup conflict. Intergroup conflict is more likely to occur in a society, like Northern Ireland, where just two major groups predominate and where the 'if you can't beat 'em join 'em' option is virtually non-existent. Of course, it is possible to be converted from one religious persuasion to another, though I suspect this is relatively rare in Northern Ireland. However, even when this does happen, Northern Ireland being a small closely-knit society it is almost impossible to escape one's roots.

So the people of Northern Ireland are locked into membership of one of two groups which will probably play a role in determining where they live, where they go to school, what games they play, and who they marry. This means that the only way to achieve a more positive social identity is to ensure that one's social group, put simply, scores points over the other social group. This therefore explains why people in Northern Ireland are apparently often more concerned with differentials (in the trade union sense) than with ultimate end goals.

Social Categorisation

So much for the theory – what of the evidence? If it is true that social categorisation occurs in all societies and that the major social categories in Northern Ireland are those of Protestant and Catholic, then there should be evidence that children are aware of the existence of these categories, perhaps from a relatively early age. This area is one of the most under-researched in relation to children in Northern Ireland. There are two main reasons for this, the most important being ethical considerations. Because there may be children in Northern Ireland innocent of the divisions in their society, the investigator must be sure that the very act of interrogating them does not in turn sensitise them to these issues (Cairns, 1980). In other words, care must be taken that it is the investigator who is learning from the research and not the children. This in turn raises a technical problem, because the would-be investigator is now faced with the problem of divising ways of examining children's awareness of the existence of the two main social categories in Northern Ireland by some indirect means. Fortunately, three investigations have been published in this area, each one using a different method to examine the question of the development of social categorisation in Northern Ireland.

If one did not know about the need for an indirect approach in this area it might seem like a rather large leap from thinking about children developing social awareness in Northern Ireland to an investigation making use of what is known to psychologists as a colour-form sorting task. However, this is exactly the task used by the first investigators in this area – Jahoda and Harrison (1975). This is a standard task, used by psychologists all over the world, which presents children with the opportunity to sort objects on the basis of either their colour or their form (shape). Studies using this task, with European and American children, have consistently revealed that as children pass from pre-school to elementary school age they display a shift from colour preference to form preference on these colour-sorting tasks.

Jahoda and Harrison, armed with this knowledge, presented their task to six and nine-year-old boys living in either a Catholic or a Protestant working-class area of Belfast, each known for its high level of sectarian feelings, and also to a comparison group of children from a Scottish city – Edinburgh (a total of 120 children). The task itself was fairly standard and consisted of sixteen geometric figures of the same size, which were made up of four different shapes (circle, square, semicircle and trapezium) with each shape appearing in one of four different colours (red, orange, blue and green). The children were asked to sort the objects into two groups and were also asked to explain how they had arrived at their particular classification. In a second stage the experimenter grouped the stimuli into different colour combinations and asked, with reference to each possible combination in turn, if the child thought the objects in each particular group went together or not.

What is significant, of course, about this is that the colours chosen by Jahoda and Harrison were the colours of the 'Protestant' flag (red and blue) and of the 'Catholic' flag (orange and green). What they wanted to see was if these colours would influence the choices of the children on the sorting task. As expected, the younger children used colour as the basis for their classification. What was remarkable was that, contrary to expectation, by age ten years the vast majority of the Belfast children (but virtually none of the Scottish children) were still classifying the objects according to colour. Further, the authors report that nearly half of the older Belfast children spontaneously mentioned the politico-religious symbolism of the colours as they carried out the task. This awareness of the symbolic meaning of the colours became even more apparent during the second stage of the task when the children were presented with all possible combinations of colours. Many of the older Belfast children said things such as 'No that's not right: you can't put Protestants with Catholics' (Jahoda and Harrison, 1975,15) or vice versa when the experimenter attempted to combine for example red and blue with green.

Of course, social categorisation in Northern Ireland although it may be applied to inanimate objects or indeed to such things as colours is primarily used by people to categorise other people. Indeed, many people in Northern Ireland claim to be highly skilled in this respect and to be able to determine another's religious group membership simply by his or her appearance. Whether this is an entirely accurate process or not is to some extent irrelevant. What is important, as Burton (1978) has pointed out is that this phenomenon – 'telling' he calls it – reveals the importance of social categorisation in Northern Ireland.

Evidence of this, as Burton observed, is the fact that encounters between strangers are dominated by 'the fundamental and almost overwhelming question, "What is he?"' (Burton, 1979).

In a series of studies reported in 1980 Cairns attempted to study one aspect of the development of this 'skill' in children in Northern Ireland – the ability to categorise first names on a denominational basis. Cairns (1980) and his colleagues began their investigation by asking a group of adults to list as many cues as possible that people used to make social categorisation on a denominational basis in Northern Ireland. This revealed that the five most commonly mentioned cues were the area where a person lives, the school they attended, their name, their appearance and the way they spoke. First names were then chosen as the stimuli to be used in further investigations with children. The next step therefore involved asking a second group of adults to list those first names which they thought were most typical of Catholic boys, Catholic girls, Protestant boys and Protestant girls. From these four lists the four most frequently mentioned names were selected for future use and these were; for Catholic males: Patrick, Sean, Seamus and Michael; for Catholic females: Mary, Bridget, Bernadette and Therese; for Protestant males: William, John, Robert and Samuel; for Protestant females: Elisabeth, Ann, Susan and Jane.

The next obvious step in the investigation was simply to ask Protestant and Catholic children at different age levels which names they thought were typically Catholic and which typically Protestant. However, because of the ethical problem noted above, a more indirect method of asking this question had to be employed. Therefore, in order to find out if children in Northern Ireland could categorise these first names on a Catholic/Protestant basis, Cairns (1980) made use of a phenomenon, familiar to psychologists who study children's and adults' memory, known as category clustering. In simple terms category clustering means that when we are presented with a list of words which we have to remember we tend to categorise or group words together if at all possible rather than try to remember them in the order in which we originally saw or heard them. For example, if we are asked to recall a list from memory such as 'cow', 'chair', 'stool', 'dog', 'table', 'horse', what we are likely to actually remember is cow, dog, horse and chair, stool, table. In other words, we categorise the list in such a way that we cluster all the animals and all the items of furniture. Among other things this tells an observer that we know that cow, dog and horse belong to one common category as do chair, stool and table.

The basic task therefore undertaken by children in the studies reported by Cairns (1980) was to listen to and/or see on a TV monitor a list of first names and then to write down (or sometimes repeat) as many of these names as possible. The list of names each child had to remember consisted of eight Catholic, eight Protestant and eight 'foreign' first names with equal numbers of male and female names within each category. The names were presented in a completely jumbled order and the foreign names were included both in an attempt to disguise the nature of the task and to control for familiarity. In a series of studies this task was presented to different groups of Catholic and Protestant children at ages ranging from five years to eleven years and standard techniques applied to determine the level of clustering, beyond that due simply to chance, which involved the three categories Protestant, Catholic and Foreign.

These revealed that while very few children can categorise first names in this way at age five years, many more (c.50 per cent) can do so at age seven years and this rises to about 70 per cent at age eleven years. Further, there was some evidence to suggest that these statistics applied equally to Catholic and Protestant children and also to suggest that the development of social categorisation, as revealed in these studies, was not influenced by whether children were locally in a denominational minority or majority.

The most remarkable feature of these results is their similarity to those obtained in the study by Jahoda and Harrison (1975). That is, two independent investigations, each using entirely different methodology and stimuli, each suggest that not till about age ten to eleven years do the majority of children in Northern Ireland learn how to categorise on a denominational basis. These results are also of some general interest because investigations in other parts of the world where racial conflicts exist have suggested that the ability to make social categorisations is probably fully developed in most children by as early as age five years. Of course, it must be remembered that a weakness of both the Cairns (1980) investigations and the Jahoda and Harrison (1975) study is that both felt obliged to employ indirect means to test their young participants' ability to make social categorisations in a Northern Irish context. This in turn raises the possibility that children in Northern Ireland may be aware of the existence of the two major social categories at a younger age than those investigators suggest but that this knowledge had not yet generalised to such things as colours or first names.

Fortunately this weakness does not bedevil a further study which has

been carried out in this area where the appropriately named investigators (McWhirter and Gamble, 1982) took the bold step of adopting
a more direct approach. In this study, which involved five to six and
nine to ten-year-old Protestants and Catholics from either an area of
active conflict or from two relatively peaceful towns (one with a large
Catholic majority, the other with a large Protestant majority) the children were asked the unambiguous questions 'What is a Protestant/
Catholic? What does Catholic/Protestant mean?' To disguise the nature
of the study slightly, however, the questions were presented in the
context of a longer word-definition test specifically designed for children. This was done by asking each child to define his/her own social
category as the third word in the test and to define the opposite term
as the last word in the test. For ethical reasons children who did not
give a clear answer were not subjected to further questioning but simply
presented with what in the jargon are referred to as non-directive
probes, such as 'Yes?' or 'Anything else?' Finally if a child at least tried
to define the other group's label then he or she was also asked if he or
she was a member of that group.

As noted earlier, religious/political differences in Northern Ireland
are something of a taboo subject (at least in 'mixed' company) akin to
talking about sex in other societies. Given this state of affairs, one
might have expected that many of the children in McWhirter and
Gamble's study would have been reluctant to respond to direct questioning about the meaning of the terms Catholic and Protestant. It is
therefore either a credit to the nature of the disguise employed by
McWhirter and Gamble or testimony to the relative maturity of the
children that less than 3 per cent showed obvious signs of tension or
unease when asked one or other of the key questions. Indeed, overall
only 28 per cent of the children failed to attempt to define at least one
of the two terms. Most of these failures were in the six-year-old group,
over half of whom offered no answer either to their own or the other
group's label.

Only four of the 96 older children similarly refused to answer. Also
some 75 per cent of the nine-year-olds offered a definition for both
terms compared with about 25 per cent of the younger children. And
not surprisingly the nine-year-olds were not only more likely to respond
but were also more likely to give more sophisticated responses. As well
as age differences, some denominational differences also occurred with
Catholic children at both ages reported to have given definitions which
were much more advanced than those of their Protestant peers. Another

interesting denominational difference was that where the children only managed to respond to one of the terms Catholic children were more likely to respond to their own group label whereas Protestant children were just as likely to attempt to define only the label Catholic as the label Protestant.

As McWhirter and Gamble (1982) note, there are obvious explanations for both these phenomena. To begin with, it is not surprising that Catholic children provide more sophisticated answers given that they generally receive more intensive religious education in the church-run schools which the vast majority of Catholic children attend. Rather more puzzling at first sight is the fact that some Protestant children appear to be as familiar with the label Catholic as with their own group label. This, however, is no doubt related to the fact that the term Protestant is actually a generic label for a group of independent churches which in Northern Ireland consists of mainly Church of Ireland, Presbyterian and Methodist.

McWhirter and Gamble did not simply note whether a child responded but also carefully recorded the actual response given by each child. This meant they were subsequently able to carry out what proved to be an illuminating detailed analysis of the children's definitions of the terms Catholic and Protestant. The surprising result of this analysis was that of the nearly 300 definitions given by the children only 5 per cent explained the terms Catholic/Protestant in relation to division or segregation in Northern Irish society – for example with reference to such things as Protestant towns or Catholic schools – while only 2 per cent defined these labels in nationalistic terms such as 'Protestant means you are not Irish' or 'Catholics are trying to win Ireland.' Indeed, in only 10 per cent of the definitions was there an explicit reference to the intergroup conflict in Northern Ireland (for example 'The army is separating Catholics from Protestants'). Further, very few of the children used value judgements, positive or negative, when defining either their own group's label or that of the other group, with the result that only 3 per cent included positive value judgements and 7 per cent negative value judgements. Put another way what this means is that six-year-old and nine-year-old children in Northern Ireland, when questioned about the meaning of the words Catholic and Protestant, virtually always offered a definition which stressed the religious aspect of these labels and shunned any political connotations.

It is just possible of course that these results are due to some methodological artefact. For example, it may be that the children simply felt themselves to be on safer ground, when answering a complete stranger, by avoiding the more sensitive side of this taboo topic. In this the children may have been aided by the way in which the questions were actually phrased. As the authors themselves note it may be significant that the key words were put to the children in their singular form and without a qualifying article – 'Protestant' and not 'the Protestants'. In fact there was a tendency noted by McWhirter and Gamble (1982), for a small number of children to stick with the singular form when talking about their own group but to slip into the plural form when talking about the other group. It may also be significant that this tendency was most marked among those children in the area where intergroup relations were at their worst.

Taken at their face value however the results of McWhirter and Gamble's (1982) study suggest that just under half of six-year-olds in Northern Ireland may be expected to understand, albeit at a relatively unsophisticated level, one or other of the terms Catholic or Protestant. Also, surprisingly, while the young Catholic child is more likely to be able to define the term 'Catholic' than the term 'Protestant', the opposite may not necessarily be true of young Protestants. Nevertheless by age nine to ten years the majority of children probably have some understanding of both terms.

These results therefore are essentially in line with those of the other two studies by Jahoda and Harrison (1975) and Cairns (1980), all three presenting a picture of children in Northern Ireland gradually developing an awareness of the two principal social categories, though the process is probably not complete until a relatively late age. At first this awareness is probably confined to the strictly religious context with, one must presume, an appreciation of the political significance of the categories emerging only later (an issue which will be taken up again in Chapter 7).

Social Identity

The next important question is at what age do children learn that they are members of one or other of the two major groups? Put more technically the question is at what age does a child in Northern Ireland develop a Catholic or a Protestant social identity? This distinction between mere group membership and social identity is important because Tajfel's theory suggests that individuals actually strive to develop a social identity, based on membership of certain groups, which eventually becomes an important aspect of the individual's self-concept. Unhappily, at the present stage in our thinking about such matters the concept of identity is a problematic one. Part of the problem is that social identity is actually a blanket term which covers the clarity of the awareness that one is a member of a group and also the strength and nature of the emotional investments that derive from this identity. In other words, when we use the term social identity we may be commenting on children's awareness that they are members of a group and/or on the fact that this membership plays an important role in their psychological make-up and/or whether membership of this particular group is positively or negatively valued.

Certainly it has been predicted on the basis of this theory (Cairns, 1982) that in a highly dichotomised society like Northern Ireland there should first exist a high level of awareness of social identity, defined in terms of the two predominant groups, and second a strong positive emotional investment in this identity. There is in fact abundant evidence that adults in Northern Ireland are well aware of, and will readily admit to, membership of one or other of the two groups. For example, in the 1971 census, in response to an optional question on denominational membership fewer than 10 per cent of the respondents choose not to answer (Darby, 1976). Once again however there are ethical problems in putting the same direct question to children. Evidence in this regard, especially from younger children, is therefore rather sparse. However, it is known that, for example, when Lawless (1981) asked nine-year-old Catholic children the simple question 'Are you a Catholic?' 94 per cent answered correctly. Similarly in the McWhirter and Gamble (1982) study, described earlier, when those children who offered a definition of the out-group label were asked if they were members of that group (that is of the other side) only two children claimed to belong to the 'wrong' group. Rather more evidence is available regarding older children. For example, Cairns and Mercer (1984) asked nearly 1,000 sixteen to seventeen-year-olds to describe themselves by choosing between a series of eighteen pairs of bipolar adjectives. Only 3 per cent failed to choose either the term Catholic or the term Protestant, rather more than those who failed to choose one of middle-class/working-class (1.8 per cent) but fewer than the 9 per cent who refused to use the more overtly political terms Republican/Loyalist.

Based on this admittedly rather sparse information, especially where younger children are concerned, it can perhaps cautiously be concluded that the process of developing awareness of one's social identity in denominational terms probably occurs in parallel with the development of the awareness of the existence of the two major social categories in Northern Ireland. In other words, as children learn about the division of Northern Irish society into two major groups they are at the same time learning to which of these groups they, and presumably their immediate family, belong.

Of particular interest is the fact that none of the research to date suggests that children in Northern Ireland are likely to misidentify themselves, that is think they belong to the other group. This may be a finding of some consequence as, in research carried out in other societies (*see* Milner, 1975 for a review), it has been claimed that minority group children are more likely to misidentify themselves in terms of group membership than are children from a group which is in the majority. As Catholics in Northern Ireland are numerically the minority group, and indeed have been equated by some (Fraser, 1974, De Paor, 1970) with the blacks in the USA, it is important to note that misidentification on the part of Catholic children has not been reported. The position is complicated however by the fact that while Catholics are in the minority in Northern Ireland they are in the majority in the whole of Ireland where it is the Protestants who form the minority group. Indeed, this line of reasoning has led Jackson (1971) to suggest that Northern Ireland's problem may be that it actually contains two minority groups. Based on the evidence reviewed here however one can only conclude that there is no case to be made that the children of either group show the psychological signs associated with minority group status. Indeed for reasons such as this it has been suggested that the problem is best thought of as involving two psychological majorities rather than two minorities (Cairns, 1982b).

While the question of children's awareness of their social identity is a relatively simple one to answer the question of the importance or salience of this identity poses a greater problem. The problem is that of finding a way to decide if a child or young person's identity as a Catholic or Protestant is something which dominates the way that child thinks about him or herself. Is it, for example, a more important aspect of self than age or gender? This difficulty is exacerbated when children are the focus of research. Nevertheless a series of studies has been carried out over the years in an attempt to throw some light on this important topic.

For example, Cairns and Mercer (1984) attempted to approach the problem by asking their adolescent respondents to rank order the eighteen adjectives they had earlier chosen to describe themselves. What this revealed was that both Catholics and Protestants were in relative agreement about the importance of most of the terms, though there was a tendency for the Catholic young people to rank the various ethno-political terms somewhat higher than did the Protestants.

Particularly interesting was the fact that when the median rank awarded to each adjective by each group was examined Catholics were found to display a tendency to rank 'Catholic' third, behind age and gender, while the Protestant trend was to rank this social identity fifth, behind age, gender, social class and religiosity (i.e. religious/not religious). Of course, central tendencies in group data as measured by such statistics as the mean or the median can conceal wide individual differences. Thus when Cairns and Mercer (1984) examined their data more closely they found that some 5 per cent of all their respondants actually ranked their denominational social identity in first place indicating that they not only felt it to be a more important self-descriptor than such things as age and gender but also more important than whether they regarded themselves as, for example, happy or unhappy and anxious or calm.

Despite the results it could still be argued that denomination social identity was not as highly rated as might have been expected given the strength of the Northern Irish conflict. After all, as has been noted 'given that almost every day people from both groups are risking their lives in situations which can only benefit their group and not themselves, then presumably it can be safely assumed that for some individuals at least, their social identity forms an important part of themselves' (Cairns, 1982, 284).

Stronger empirical evidence to support this observation has in fact been supplied by Weinreich (1982). Over a number of years, Weinreich (1980) has developed a theoretical framework, Identity Structure Analysis, which combines a psychodynamic concept of identity, for example from the work of Erckson (1968), with elements from personal construct psychology (Kelly, 1955). This in turn has allowed him to produce a computer linked technique – IDEX for identity exploration – in order to attempt to measure identity structure within individuals. Using this sophisticated methodology Weinreich (1982) carried out a detailed analysis of the personal and social identities of 160 adolescents (fifteen to sixteen years) both Protestants and Catholics, boys and girls, who at the time of the study (1981) were attending four schools in Belfast all segregated by religion and by sex. To provide the basic data required by the IDEX program each individual was asked to rate aspects not only of his or her self-concept but also of others ranging from 'same sex parent' to 'the IRA'. The ratings were made using bipolar constructs which included two related to nationality ('Irish'/'not at all Irish' and 'British'/'not at all British') and two related to religion ('Protestant'/'not at all Protestant' plus 'Catholic'/'not at all Catholic').

One of the claims of Identity Structure Analysis is that it is able to produce, in numerical form, an indication of 'the evaluative consistency with which people use their constructs to evaluate themselves and their social world' (Weinreich, 1982). In other words, to estimate the extent to which a person's identity is organised around particular ideas or constructs. According to Weinreich his study in Belfast revealed that for both the Catholic and Protestant young people who took part 'national allegiance and religious affiliation combine together as core evaluative dimensions of their identities' so that 'their evaluations of their social world are dominated by these criteria over and beyond all others' (Weinreich, 1982).

Weinreich's IDEX approach is relatively new and so its use has sadly been confined to this one study in a Northern Irish context. Also, this approach, as it stands at the moment, is unsuitable for use with younger children. Where younger children are concerned a much simpler approach has therefore been adopted which has usually entailed asking children to write or talk about themselves or perhaps to complete a variation of Kuhn and McPartland's (1954) Twenty Statements test. This simply consists of the question 'Who am I?' followed by twenty sentences, each beginning 'I am. . . .' which must be completed using a different self-descriptor each time. The basic idea behind this approach is to see if the child mentions a particular social identity at all or perhaps to see where in the list of self-descriptors a particular item gets a mention. The idea here is that a social identity which is mentioned first on, for example, the Twenty Statements test, must be a more salient identity for that person than one which gets mentioned twentieth or indeed not at all.

Trew (1981a) asked a group of 278 first year university students and final year secondary school children to 'Write as much as possible in answer to the question "What are you?".' When this was done the surprising result was that only 8 per cent of these young people spontaneously referred to their religious denomination in describing themselves. In a second part of the questionnaire they were then asked to provide information as to their age, sex and religion. With this form of questioning 93 per cent were willing to label themselves as either Catholic or Protestant. Further, when Trew examined the self descriptions each young person had provided more closely she found that only two had mentioned their religious denomination in the first sentence. For example, Trew (1983) cites one young man who managed to mention twenty-two different things about himself with the fact that he was a Protestant not emerging till he had mentioned seventeen other, presumably more important, facts.

As Trew (1983), who has reviewed the work in this area notes, one possible explanation for these results could be that these techniques tend to focus on what could be considered personal identity as opposed to social identity. This means that when children, for example, are asked to complete the twenty 'I am. . . .' sentences they often respond with (along with such things as age and gender) facts such as 'a good footballer' or 'bad at English' (Ross, 1981). In an attempt to examine this methodological explanation for the contrary results from Trew's (1981) study and that of Weinreich (1982), Mullan (1982) asked 100 first year university students to complete the Twenty Statements Test while a further 100 were asked to answer the question 'As members of what groups or categories of people would you like to count yourself?' Contrary to the hypothesis originally entertained the second form of questioning did not increase the number of respondants who mentioned their denominational social identity.

A further problem as Cairns and Mercer (1984) have pointed out, is that most of the measurement techniques employed do not really do justice to the concept of social identity as presented in Tajfel's theory. A particular weakness is that social identity in that theory is envisaged as a dynamic entity which may vary from time to time and from situation to situation. Some evidence that this may be so is presented by Trew (1981b) who tested some 600 Catholic children aged nine years and eleven years from a particularly militant area of Northern Ireland in 1981. Either by accident or design the study was carried out during a period in the recent history of Northern Ireland when sectarian feelings were particularly strong – the time at which the Republican Prisoners' hunger strike was at its height. Indeed, Trew (1983) reports that one of the hunger strikers had just been buried with full Republican military honours in the village in which one of the eight schools taking part in the study was located. And sure enough, her results reveal something of an upsurge in the salience of social identity in response to a modified version of the Twenty Statements Test, this time asking the question

'What are you?' Now some 46 per cent of the children spontaneously referred to themselves as Catholics with significantly more eleven-year-olds doing so than nine-year-olds.

Trew (1983) concludes her review of work in this area by noting that 'although Northern Ireland is a divided society the Protestant/ Catholic dichotomy does not necessarily pervade individual self-perception. . . .' (p.199). To this could be added that a combination of factors both external to the individual, such as the current political climate, as well as the micro-situation the individual finds him or herself in, plus internal factors such as age and denominational allegiance, can and almost certainly do act together to increase the salience of social identity in denominational terms in Northern Ireland. In one important respect this evidence is in accord with that from other societies, particularly the USA, where research has tended to suggest that for minority group children social identity as a minority group member is more likely to be a salient feature of self-perception.

Paradoxically, the research in the USA has also suggested that while black children may be more aware of their identity, they are also more likely to show signs of rejecting that identity (Milner, 1975). Indeed, based on this experience other researchers have tended to assume that the possession of a negatively-valued social identity is in fact a characteristic common to all minority group children in all societies. In turn it has also been assumed that a concomitant of this negative social identity is a low level of self-esteem among minority group children when compared with majority group children. Certainly for some time it was accepted that the empirical evidence favoured this view, with studies producing supporting data not just from minority group children in the USA but also New Zealand and indeed Great Britain (*see* Milner, 1975, for a review). Recently, however, this idea has been the target of striking criticisms (Nobles, 1973; Banks, 1976). What these and other critics have pointed out is that many of the studies which have claimed to demonstrate lowered self-esteem among black children, especially in the USA, did so on the basis of rather tangential evidence and without actually measuring self-esteem directly. Instead these claims, it appears, had often been based on an interpretation of tests of racial identification. That is it was argued that because minority group children misidentified their group membership they must also have a low opinion of themselves. When more recent studies in the USA examined black children directly, however, they failed to find any evidence that they possess consistently lower levels of self-esteem than white children.

One positive outcome from this is that researchers have begun to think more carefully about the relationship between the way individuals evaluate their own group and the way they evaluate themselves. The major result of this rethink has been the realisation that the relationship between these two need not be a perfect correlation. In other words, there is not necessarily a direct link between one's personal identity and one's social identity. On most occasions an individual's ideas about him or herself will be influenced by daily interaction with others from the same social group as much, if not more, than by the larger society. Thus, as Tajfel (1978) has observed, it is possible to remain happy and contented in a ghetto.

Cairns (1982b) has reviewed evidence based on observations by social anthropologists, historians and other social scientists which has led him to conclude that both groups in Northern Ireland, Catholics and Protestants, appear to possess 'relatively positive social identities.' Certainly there appears to be little doubt that Protestants not only enjoy a positive social identity today but probably always have done – at least for the last two or three hundred years. For the Catholics of Northern Ireland Cairns (1982b) suggests a positive social identity may have been a relatively more recent phenomenon (perhaps of the late nineteenth century) and further that the evidence available indicates that even today Catholics may evaluate their social identity in a some-what equivocal way. This statement has to be surrounded by a number of 'ifs' and 'buts' because at the time Cairns was writing his review, the early 1980s, only one study was available which actually provided any empirical evidence on this point. This was a study by O'Donnell (1977) who had collected information on the words used by Northern Irish Catholic and Protestant adults to describe their own group (and the other group) and the way in which these words were evaluated. What O'Donnell (1977) reports is that in his particular study the ten words most frequently chosen by Protestants to describe their own group were subsequently rated by them as positive rather than neutral or negative. On the other hand, of the ten words most frequently chosen by Catholics to describe their group only six were considered to be positive while the remaining four were actually rated negatively – these were 'long-suffering', 'insecure', 'deprived' and 'unfortunate'.

One of the big advantages researchers in the area of intergroup conflict in racial societies have is that it is much easier to work with children. This is because, whether for ethical reasons or because children may be so young as to be illiterate, it is relatively easy in racial settings to find stimuli which will represent the groups in conflict. For example, in the USA there is no need to worry about asking children if they are black or white instead one can simply show them a photograph of a black and a white child or a pair of dolls, one black the other white and ask the question 'Which one of these is most like you?' and indeed most of the research literature in this area is based on endless variations on this technique. In Northern Ireland things are rather more difficult. However, as noted earlier, Cairns (1980) reported that people in Northern Ireland do claim to be able to tell whether a person is a Catholic or a Protestant by, among other things, looking at the person's face. Stringer (1984) made use of this fact to develop a set of photographs which could be used as stimuli in studies in Northern Ireland in a similar way to the black and white photographs employed in racial studies in the USA. To do this he began with a large number of photographs of male faces (over 100) and asked adults to rate these on a scale from 'very Protestant' to 'very Catholic'. Using this procedure he was able to identify ten faces which both Catholics and Protestants in Northern Ireland almost always considered to be 'Protestant' faces and ten which were almost always considered to be 'Catholic' faces. Stringer and Cairns (1983) then made use of this set of stereotyped faces to investigate the way in which older children (fourteen to fifteen-year-olds) in Northern Ireland evaluate their group. The children saw the twenty faces one at a time presented on a video screen. Each face was exposed for a few seconds and then the children were asked to rate that face on a set of nine bipolar adjectives such as good/bad or light/heavy. These adjectives in turn were used to produce three main scores representing a physical potency factor, a social potency factor and a general evaluation factor. In support of O'Donnell's (1977) finding Stringer and Cairns (1983) report that the Protestant children rated the stereotyped 'Protestant' faces more highly than they did the stereotyped 'Catholic' faces on all three scales. The Catholics in turn agreed with the Protestants and also rated the 'Catholic' faces lower but only on the social potency and physical potency scales. On the general evaluation scale Catholics scored the 'Catholic' faces as equal to the 'Protestant' faces thus giving them a significantly higher score than they had been given by the Protestant children on that scale. One interpretation of these results is that once again they demonstrate that Protestants possess a definite positive social identity while Catholics also evaluate their social identity positively but in a less clear-cut way. Incidentally

Stringer and Cairns (1983) feel that the results of their study may also provide some insight into the question of how minority groups in general evaluate their own group. The current confusion concerning whether minority group children in particular will always possess a negative social identity may, they suggest, be because investigators have tended to use only one evaluative dimension at a time. The Stringer and Cairns (1983) study instead makes the point that for minority group members evaluation of their group is not an all or none phenomenon but rather that minority in-group attitudes are complex and multi-dimensional. In addition Stringer and Cairns (1983) were at pains to point out that individual young Catholics are not expected to possess poorer *self*-concepts than do young Protestants simply because they may not evaluate their social identity as Catholics in Northern Ireland in a totally positive way.

The reports by both O'Donnell (1977) and Stringer and Cairns (1983) showing that Catholic young people (and indeed adults) in Northern Ireland may be rather more ambivalent in their evaluation of their social identity also finds echoes in the study by Weinreich (1982) described earlier. Weinreich examined, among other things, the extent to which what he refers to as 'identity conflicts' occurred in his sample. Identification conflicts he defines as those conflicts which emerge when an individual empathically identifies with another and yet at the same time wishes to dissociate him or herself from certain of the other person's characteristics. He reports that, compared to his Protestant respondants, the young Catholics who took part in his study showed more evidence of identification conflicts *with their own group*. This appears to indicate therefore that in social identity terms young Catholics wish to think of themselves as part of their own group but only to a limited extent. At the same time, they think also of themselves as different from the Catholic group – at least in certain important ways. All of this would appear to make sound psychological sense. If, as the studies of O'Donnell (1977) and Stringer and Cairns (1983) indicate, Catholics see their group as possessing both positive and negative attributes, then it is only to be expected that individual Catholics would, while recognising this state of affairs, see themselves as possessing the positive but not the negative characteristics of a 'typical' Northern Irish Catholic.

Social Psychological Distinctiveness

Individuals, according to Tajfel's theory, wish to achieve a positive social identity but can only do this (in highly stratified and inflexible societies like Northern Ireland) not by their individual efforts but by ensuring that their own group comes out on top when social comparisons between groups are made. Once again, there is very little empirical evidence available as to the way in which the groups in Northern Ireland do this. Tajfel (1978) suggests that acting in terms of the group is the only way to account for 'the many examples of selfless actions or even extreme sacrifice for the sake of a group', actions which clearly have no utilitarian value where the individual is concerned. Sadly Northern Ireland is all too familiar with such behaviour ranging from the dramatic acts of the Republican hunger strikers to the equally courageous behaviour of loyalists in lonely border farms who refuse to be intimidated from their homes. Even on a more everyday level the flag-flying and marching for which Northern Ireland has become a byword on television screens throughout the world probably plays an important role here. Weinreich (1982), who, it should perhaps be noted, does not approach the question of social identity in Catholics and Protestants from a Tajfelian perspective, nevertheless does provide some insights which support this interpretation of intergroup conflict in Northern Ireland. In particular he notes that his results suggest that *both* Catholic and Protestant adolescents reveal identification conflicts with the other group. What this amounts to, Weinreich suggests, is in fact a 'pressure to disassociate' from the other group which in turn results in a *tendency to exaggerate differences* between the groups. This is of course exactly what Tajfel's theory predicts will happen in any intergroup conflict. This also helps to account for the fact that outside observers are often struck not by the differences between the groups in Northern Ireland but by the similarities. For example, both are European, Christian, English-speaking and live on the same small island, to mention but a few! Nevertheless in reality it is the differences which are focussed upon by the Northern Irish people themselves, not the similarities. In fact Cairns (1983b) has even gone so far as to suggest that these differences are not simply exaggerated but that there exists a desire to *create* differences. It is this desire to foster differences, this emphasis upon the 'social construction of ethnicity' (Cairns, 1982b) which he suggests may be behind such innocent practices as the desire to give one's children a distinctive first name which will clearly label them as Protestant or

Catholic for life. This Cairns (1983b) suspects, is a relatively recent practice (post First World War) which could be of considerable importance as an index of parental attitudes and their later implications for child rearing in Northern Ireland. After all, as Seeman (1976) has pointed out, psychologists have long recognised the importance of parental attitudes while the child is growing up. Might it not be therefore that the names given to a child at birth are in fact 'an index of initial attitudes and expectations' determined even before child-parent interactions begin? And this desire to create differences, particularly where children are concerned, continues throughout the formative years, the most obvious example being the insistence that children not only grow up in segregated housing estates but above all attend separate schools (again a relatively recent phenomenon).

Conclusions

The categories involved in taking sides in Northern Ireland are conceptually quite complex. No doubt this, plus the absence of obvious visual cues, accounts for the fact that in the main children in Northern Ireland appear to be somewhat older than children in racially dominated societies before they develop an awareness of these categories. Further, to begin with at least, the evidence to date suggests that children's knowledge of these categories relates more to their religious significance than to their socio-political significance. This late development of social awareness in socio-political terms in Northern Ireland may be particularly significant. Its significance lies in the fact that one would predict that it *should* be easier to prevent the social awareness which develops later, rather than earlier, taking on the status of a rigid all-or-none category and thus becoming the basis for later intergroup conflict.

When this awareness does begin to emerge, however, it appears that children also begin to learn to identify with their own particular group. The evidence is less clear that identification with one's own group readily becomes an important aspect of the way in which a vast majority of the children in Northern Ireland think about themselves. This process undoubtedly varies, with Catholic children more likely to view their social identity as important and the salience of social identity increases with age and among those children living in areas where intergroup conflict is particularly overt. On the other hand it is just possible that this failure on the part of the research to date, to demonstrate the overwhelming importance of social identity for children in Northern

Ireland, may be telling us more about the methodological problems which attend research in this area than about the objective situation. My guess is that anyone who lives in Northern Ireland would probably agree that while one's social identity may not always be to the forefront of one's consciousness it is nevertheless never far away. Weinreich (1982) suggests that because both Protestants and Catholics are so keen to establish that they are different from each other this means that, paradoxically, their attention will be drawn continually to the 'offending group'. Therefore, he suggests that although people in Northern Ireland may be 'disinclined consciously to devote much thought to the other group', at the same time they will experience the other group 'obtruding into their consciousness as a matter of their own personal identity.'

Most of the time, however, a child in Northern Ireland – perhaps more so than an adult – will find him or herself in situations which will be more likely to 'switch on' personal identity rather than social identity. Therefore, the fact that current research suggests Catholics may have a less obviously positive social identity than Protestants need not mean that Catholic children at all times think less highly of themselves simply because they are Catholics. The evidence from this area of research, despite the fact that it is relatively meagre, may in fact be significant beyond its immediate psychological context. This is because researchers from other disciplines have suggested that Northern Ireland's conflict may be remarkable because it is between two minority groups not simply a majority and a minority. There is however nothing in the psychological evidence to reinforce this suggestion. Actually, if anything the evidence is more likely to reinforce the suggestion that the Northern Irish conflict is one between two *majority* groups (Cairns, 1982b, Poole, 1983). Often the terms minority and majority are used as short hand for the terms inferior and superior respectively. However, it should be remembered that groups' roles in this context are not necessarily fixed. One possible interpretation of the present situation in Northern Ireland therefore is that the Catholic group has been growing in stature while the Protestant group has come more and more under attack. In social identity terms this would mean that the way the Catholic group evaluates its social identity is becoming more and more positive. This, almost by definition, means of course that the Protestant group's identity has become increasingly threatened. Therefore, while the information reviewed here describes the situation in the late 1970s and early 1980s it does not describe a static situation but rather provides a snapshot of one point in a continuing struggle between two groups. The important point is that one group attaining a sense of superiority at the other group's expense will not lead to a peaceful solution of the conflict but instead ensure its perpetuation.

6

Schools in Northern Ireland

'Ulster Education Passes Parents' Test' was the claim in a banner head-line in the principal Northern Irish newspaper, the *Belfast Telegraph* in November 1984. This confident assertion was based on the results of a survey, commissioned by the newspaper, of 228 parents. The survey had revealed that, in response to the question 'How satisfied are you overall with your child's education?' 56 per cent had replied 'very satis-fied' and 39 per cent 'quite satisfied' – in all a total of 95 per cent apparently satisfied customers of the Northern Irish educational system. And it would seem that Northern Irish parents have good reason to be content with the educational performance of their schools, according to Harbison (1983), who has briefly reviewed some of the data available in this area, a series of surveys carried out by the National Foundation for Educational Research. These have shown that both in the primary and the secondary sectors children in Northern Ireland 'are achieving educational standards which are above the level of most of the English regions and Wales, only rivalled by the South of England' (Harbison, 1983, 7). This, as Harbison notes, is all the more remarkable because these surveys usually reveal that, in general, areas with the lowest economic levels tend to produce the worst educational performance. Northern Ireland is apparently an exception to this rule, having some of the worst socio-economic conditions and yet is near the top in terms of educational attainment as measured in this survey.

What this rosy picture conceals however is that at another level everyone is not totally satisfied with the educational system in Northern Ireland. In fact education has been the target of persistent criticisms from a vocal minority for at least the last ten to fifteen years. These criticisms have centred around one major issue – the existence of two separate religious school systems and their possible role in perpetuating, if not creating, the basis for intergroup conflict in Northern Ireland.

The Separate Systems

It says something about Northern Irish society in general that this segregation along religious lines in education is barely acknowledged in official circles. Instead the legal position is that Northern Ireland has indeed two educational systems but these are referred to as the controlled sector and the voluntary sector. The controlled sector is, as its name suggests, totally financed and controlled by the government of Northern Ireland through the medium of local boards. The voluntary or maintained sector, on the other hand, is only partially financed from tax payers' funds with 15 per cent of approved capital expenditure having to be found from other sources. In practice what this actually means is that the public or controlled sector is virtually one hundred per cent Protestant while the 'semi-private' voluntary sector is predominantly Catholic. As Darby *et al* (1977) point out:

> the most convincing contemporary demonstration of the existence of denominational education, at least in primary schools, is the fact that when a new maintained primary school is being planned the government deals directly with the Catholic Church. On the other hand when a new controlled primary school has been built, the Protestant churches only are invited to provide nominees to its management committee.

Thus, as they note, the controlled primary schools are *de facto* Protestant schools and at one level at least government acknowledges this.

A further indication of the sensitivity of government on this topic is that it is difficult to obtain hard information as to the actual levels of segregation in the school system. This despite (Darby *et al.*, 1977) the publication by the government of *Education Statistics* which presents relevant information broken down according to age and sex but not by religion. One of the few estimates of the extent of segregation is Barritt and Carters' (1962) guestimate that at least 98 per cent of all Catholic primary school children at that time attended Catholic primary schools. Certainly authorities in the field seem to agree that, whatever the precise level, segregation in education is almost total, particularly at the primary or elementary level (Akenson, 1973; Darby, 1976).

The way in which societies school their children is 'culturally diagnostic' according to Akenson (1973) who has written the authoritative work on the history of the battle for the control of schools in Northern

Ireland. And the significance of segregation in these schools perhaps takes on a clearer meaning when one realises that this segregation is not simply a reflection of segregation in other areas of life in Northern Ireland. For example, it might be assumed that segregation in residential housing means that children only have to attend their neighbourhood school for segregation in education to follow. However, Poole (1982) who has examined patterns of segregation in housing in Northern Ireland comments that 'nowhere is housing segregation as intense as the religious segregation in the schools.' Instead, he calculates that while most of the population of Northern Ireland live in fairly segregated areas, mostly in the larger towns, the majority of towns actually have a low level of religious segregation.

It can only be concluded therefore that religious segregation in education is self-imposed and in particular is the result of what Darby (1976) has referred to as 'the deep rooted suspicion of Catholics towards state control of their schools.' It is perhaps for this very reason – that segregation in Northern Irish schools does not simply reflect the division in other walks of life but rather magnifies it – that the dual education system has come to be seen by many as, if not the cause of division in Northern Irish society at least a major perpetuating factor.

The Promise Of Integration

In the present context it is particularly interesting to note that of the two books written to date about Northern Ireland which adopt what can be loosely described as a 'psychological perspective' both advocate integrated education as a cure or at least one of the cures for Northern Ireland's ills (Fraser, 1974; Heskin, 1980b). Fraser (1974) in particular adopts a very militant stance on this issue devoting a whole chapter in his book *Children in Conflict* to the role of the school systems in the conflict in Northern Ireland. In this chapter, entitled, 'Education for Aggro', he claims that the role of segregated schooling in perpetuating the conflict is widely recognised and that integrating schools, at least at the primary level, is 'the one initiative that would contribute more than any other single factor to the prospect of peace in Ulster' (p. 164). Indeed, he goes so far as to assert that while segregation in education continues to exist episodes of community strife will continue in Northern Ireland. Heskin (1980b) has presented a more reasoned argument in favour of integrated education and framed in less strident tones. But in the end he too reaches conclusions similar to those of Fraser. In particular he claims that because of the nature of society in Northern Ireland and the way it differs from, for example, the USA, one can be optimistic about the results of school integration in Northern Ireland despite equivocal results from other societies. To be fair to Heskin, and indeed to other writers on this topic, he does make it clear that he is not naively assuming that integrated schools will heal Northern Ireland's wounds overnight, nor is he suggesting that contact *per se* whether in schools or elsewhere is all that is required. Nevertheless he does conclude that, at a social level, the introduction of integrated schooling is 'the single potentially most helpful step' (Heskin, 1980b).

If this is so, why does segregated education continue? Is it because the people of Northern Ireland, or at least a majority of them, wish it to continue? The answer to this last question has been sought in a number of surveys (seven since 1967) usually carried out by professional pollsters and frequently commissioned by newspapers or magazines. For example, in 1973 a local magazine, *Fortnight*, commissioned a poll which asked 'How would you feel about your child, or children you know, going to a school attended by pupils and taught by teachers some of whom were Catholic and some Protestant?' The results mirrored those of similar earlier exercises in the late sixties in that a majority were in favour (62 per cent) with only a small minority (13 per cent) against – the remainder were 'don't knows' etc. And more recently, in 1981 when the British newspaper the *Sunday Times* asked 'Do you think Catholic and Protestant children should go to the same schools?' again an overwhelming majority – 72 per cent – answered 'yes'.

On the face of it this seems to indicate that a clear majority of people in Northern Ireland would support a move towards the integration of schools – and yet some nagging doubts remain! If these polls are to be believed how does one explain the storm that erupted in 1977 when plans were announced for a Catholic and Protestant school, not to merge, but simply to share the same canteen building, though at different times so that the two sets of children would never have come into actual physical contact. Or the protests that greeted (and finally squashed) the proposal not to integrate schools but only to retain the separate Catholic and Protestant teacher training colleges as segregated institutions but on the same campus. One possible answer is that it is the churches who are to blame for the fact that the *status quo* is maintained. Heskin (1980b) is more specific and places the responsibility for the continuation of segregation firmly on the shoulders of the Catholic hierarchy. Certainly the Catholic church has always been adamant that Catholic children must be educated within 'the Catholic ethos' which in practice means if possible in separate schools staffed by Catholic teachers. Akenson (1973) notes however that despite their other differences, the church leaders both Protestant *and* Catholic, seem united in their opposition to integration. One cynical interpretation therefore could be that integrated education has not come to Northern Ireland because the decision lies in the hands of those 'with an interest in maintaining numbers in the pews' (Fraser, 1974). More recently, however, both the Presbyterian and the Church of Ireland have at least expressed support for experiments in integrated education.

Divided Schools?

A remarkable feature of this debate has been that until recently it has been dominated by rhetoric and opinions with no empirical evidence forthcoming from either side. The study by Darby and his colleagues (1977), *Education and Community in Northern Ireland: Schools Apart?* was therefore a pioneering effort designed to examine the similarities and differences between the two systems. As noted earlier one of the principal arguments for the retention of segregated schools has been that of the Catholic church which has insisted that Catholic children where possible attend Catholic schools. A corollary to this argument must be that the existing Catholic and Protestant schools differ because, after all, one presumably is imbued with the 'Catholic ethos' while the other is not. But what does this mean in practice? How do the two sets of schools actually differ – in terms of their organisation, their links with the community, religious practices within the schools or in matters relating to the curriculum or extra-curricular activities? These are some of the many issues that the *Schools Apart* (Darby *et al.*, 1977) study set out to examine.

This was done by sending a questionnaire to schools throughout Northern Ireland, sampled in such a way as to make them representative of (a) all districts in Northern Ireland, (b) both sides of the religious divide and (c) both primary and secondary levels of education. In effect therefore the study, which was carried out early in 1976, sampled some 13 per cent of all primary schools in Northern Ireland and just over 30 per cent of all secondary schools. The response rate was reasonable with about 60 per cent of both primary and secondary schools responding – although this conceals the fact that at the secondary level the more academically oriented (that is the grammar schools) were much less likely to respond than their less academically inclined colleagues. This snapshot of the 'big picture' in Northern Ireland was also supplemented by a more detailed examination of the denominational educational systems in one small area. Here the data were gathered using interviews with school principals, teachers, parents and representatives of management committees connected with some eighteen schools.

It came as no surprise of course when Darby *et al.* (1977) reported that 'Protestant and Roman Catholic school children in Northern Ireland attend schools where their co-religionists predominate.' In fact, what the study revealed was that possibly as many as 70 per cent of Northern Ireland's schools are exclusively attended by children from only one denomination. The study also indicated however that the predominantly Catholic schools are much more exclusive than the predominantly Protestant schools. For example, 90 per cent of Catholic primary schools in the survey contained not a single non-Catholic child in comparison to 67 per cent of the Protestant primary schools which were 100 per cent Protestant. Similarly, some 3 per cent of Protestant primary schools reported that somewhere between 10 and 19 per cent of their pupils were Catholics, whereas no Catholic school reported that they contained a similar level of non-Catholic children.

More startling was the degree of segregation among teachers. This information is particularly striking when translated into actual numbers, revealing for example that of the 2,751 teachers in the schools sampled only 41 taught in schools where they were in the minority in religious terms. Again, as with pupils, this trend was particularly marked in the primary sector.

Aside from these dramatic, but not entirely unexpected differences, the rest of the report is notable because of the similarities it uncovered between the two denominational school systems in Northern Ireland. For example, the educational qualifications of the teachers were relatively similar as were the work profiles of the principals in terms of the proportion of their time spent on administration, teaching, etc. The forms of discipline used in both types of school revealed a common approach too, although there was a suggestion that the predominantly Catholic schools might be somewhat more punishment oriented. In this respect, however, it is interesting to note that Darby *et al.* (1977) suggest that in both school systems the general picture was one of a 'traditional' rather than 'liberal' approach.

Two areas in which differences might have been expected to emerge were religious practices in school and sporting activities. In the question-naire a total of five questions examined religious activities and teaching of religion and the authors note that in general the answers revealed 'high conformity of practice within both categories of schools.' Sport has for some time been considered to be one of the many forms of social behaviour which are divided along denominational lines. In general, under the influence of the Gaelic Athletic Association (GAA), which until recently prohibited its members from playing 'British' games (for example soccer, rugby, hockey and cricket), traditional Irish games (for example, Gaelic football and camogie) have flourished. And here the report reveals that, as expected, no Protestant schools played Gaelic (Irish) games while no Catholic school played cricket and few played rugby or hockey. It is important to note, however, that the authors also highlighted the fact that there is a considerable number of sports 'which cut across the denominational split', including soccer, tennis, netball and basketball.

Yet whether these sports are actually used to cross the divide is debat-able. Certainly, the *Schools Apart* report makes the point that it was very rare for teachers to visit each other's schools and as a consequence, very little was known about the day to day running of each other's schools. Indeed, they suggest there exists a degree of mutual suspicion between the two systems. Protestant teachers were particularly wary of what they saw as the major influence of the Catholic clergy in the Catholic schools while Catholic teachers feared integration because they saw it, in effect, as a take-over of the Catholic school system. The *Schools Apart* report did however suggest that while there was little support for an integrated educational system, at least in the near future, there was a constructive concern to improve relationships within the existing separate systems.

One other study in this area has adopted an unusual approach; over a period of one year Murray (1982) acted as participant-observer in two Northern Irish primary schools, one Catholic the other Protestant. His conclusions are very similar to those reached by Darby *et al.* (1977) – with one notable exception. Murray suggests that where religious instruction was concerned there were differences between the two schools both in terms of the content and the general approach. In particular he reports that in the Catholic school more emphasis was given to religious instruction to the extent that at certain times of the year this subject took precedence over all other subjects – for example when a class was being prepared for First Communion. In the Protestant school, in contrast, religious instruction was strictly confined to what he refers to as the 'non-secular' day, that is between about 9.00 a.m. and 9.45 a.m. when morning assembly, prayers, etc. would be held. Apart from this one major difference, however, he reports (Murray, 1983) 'that at a curricular level the schools were almost indistinguishable.'

If observers such as Darby and his colleagues are correct in suggesting that Protestant and Catholic schools differ little in the way they teach basic subjects then one would expect to find few differences in the educational attainments of their pupils. This by and large is the conclusion reached by Harbison (1980), who reviewed evidence available from schools in the Belfast area in the 1970s concerned with such things as reading attainment, verbal reasoning performance and teacher rated behavioural maladjustment. The results of these comparisons revealed few if any differences which could be related to whether children attended a Protestant or a Catholic school.

On the few occasions when such differences did emerge they were slight and one could not be sure that they were due to denominational differences *per se* or related to the fact that Catholic children are more likely to come from poorer socio-economic backgrounds. More recently a government publication (PPRU Monitor, No. 2., 1985) has added further information in this area. As a result of a survey of some 11,000 people aged sixteen-plus in Northern Ireland it was reported that Protestant respondents were more likely to have stayed on at school beyond the elementary level and very slightly more had gone on to university or polytechnic. Once again, however, these differences are more likely to be due to differences in the socio-economic structure of the two groups rather than the separate educational systems *per se* and we can conclude that when it comes to what may be broadly described as the 'three Rs' both school systems are equally successful.

Indeed, in one important respect the Catholic school system may be surpassing the Protestant one, according to Murray and Osborne (1983). They reason that because a greater proportion of the children attending Catholic schools are from working-class homes, and because evidence from all over the western world indicates that working-class children do less well at school than the middle class, it therefore follows that the gap between Protestant and Catholic educational attainment in Northern Ireland should be greater than it actually is. If anything, therefore, this means the Catholic school system's record of achievement for the children of the working class may be better than that of the Protestant school system.

Despite, or indeed because of, the evidence from Darby and his colleagues that the two school systems are remarkably alike and the further evidence that both are equally successful, critics of segregated education are less than likely to be convinced that the existence of these separate schools does not add to the divisions in the greater society. On the other hand, it could be argued that not enough emphasis has been laid on the differences between the two systems which, though small, may yet be significant. It could also be suggested that researchers have concentrated rather too much on quantitative differences between Catholic and Protestant schools and not enough on the qualitative differences.

Language is important in ethnic group relations because it is very often 'a criterial attribute of ethnic group membership, a cue for inter-ethnic categorisation, and can readily become a primary symbol of ethnicity. . .' according to Giles and Johnston (1983). Indeed, because of the emotional significance of language for ethnic groups one often finds language issues at the focal point of inter-ethnic conflicts. Yet despite the fact that scholars in many parts of the world have recognised the role of language in inter-ethnic conflicts virtually no research appears to have been done on this topic in Northern Ireland. This is a glaring omission because one significant difference between the two school systems in Northern Ireland is that virtually all Catholic secondary level schools teach the Irish language, often as a compulsory subject, while no Protestant schools do so. The importance of this goes beyond the mere learning of another language, because the Irish language and its revival is seen by many as central to the revival of Irish culture in general. Indeed, the nationalism which led to the foundation of the Republic of Ireland owed much of its early momentum to the language movement which began in the late nineteenth and early twentieth centuries. Thus in 1922 the Constitution of the then 'Irish Free State' recognised Irish as the national language and made it compulsory in schools there, a status it retains today. The Irish language remains a potent symbol of nationalism (and republicanism) today, recognised by many as a barrier to the unification of Ireland because, in the words of a Prime Minister of the Republic of Ireland 'What to a majority of the Irish people has become sacred is to the Northern Protestant today an alien and even hateful tradition' (Fitzgerald, 1972). Despite this – or perhaps because of it – the Irish language has undergone something of a revival among Catholics in Northern Ireland. Today it appears to be flourishing if not in the schools at least outside them judging by the number of people enrolling for adult Irish language classes. Further, after sixty plus years of the existence of the Northern jurisdiction the government has just recognised the first ever primary school where Irish is the medium for all instruction and the state-run radio service, Radio Ulster, a subsidiary of the BBC, has begun a short weekly Irish language programme. It is, of course, important to note that (as in the Republic) few people would assert that Irish is their first language or would even claim to be fluent in Irish. Nevertheless it is also important to recognise, as Giles and Johnston (1983) point out that it is not necessary for an ethnic group to speak the language in order for it to become a symbol of their identity.

Irish is almost certainly the only subject which does not cross the denominational divide in education in Northern Ireland. Further, in those Catholic schools in which it is taught it undoubtedly takes up but a small proportion of the school day, competing as it must with the many subjects that are common to both school systems. Of course, as many have pointed out (for example Darby, 1976, Malone, 1973) what is critical is not simply the content of a school lesson but the way in which the material is taught. This is what Malone (1973) refers to as a school's 'hidden political agenda'. In other words, the conscious or unconscious 'assumptions and allegiances' which may be transmitted by the teacher particularly via the medium of such subjects as literature, art, music and history. The role of these subjects as a potentially divisive force in education appears to have escaped critical examination – except, that is, for the more obvious question of history teaching. Even here the 'research' has largely been confined to examining the content of school textbooks peculiar to either the Protestant or Catholic school systems. Those who have carried out such examinations (for example Barritt and Carter, 1962; Akenson, 1973) appear to agree that there exists an extensive but subtle bias in the way these texts cover Irish history. The considered opinion is that in the Catholic schools Irish history is taught with a certain emotional emphasis upon Anglo-Irish relations. In particular there tends to be an emphasis upon Ireland's historic struggle against the oppressor (the English). Darby (1974) provides the following illustration of this from a textbook published in 1960:

> Ireland is only a small country but her strength is based on things spiritual, and because of her long fight for freedom and justice and her loyalty to the Christian traditions, she holds an honoured place amongst the nations.

Protestant schools, on the other hand, tend to teach British history which means that Ireland is, if not ignored, certainly relegated to a secondary role while the emphasis is always upon English history. Further, English attitudes towards Ireland and the Irish are never far from the surface despite attempts to supress them. For example, from a typical British textbook of the 1960s: 'In those days Ireland was known as the "Isle of Saints"' followed a few sentences later by 'A district round Dublin, called the "English Pale", was ruled by the English, but the rest of the land with its bogs was wild and backward.'

Despite all this, any examination of the two school systems must in the end conclude that, while some differences exist, the similarities far outweigh the differences. Are the differences therefore important? Darby (1976) suggests that what must be recognised is 'the cumulative effect' of these differences which although perhaps 'insignificant in themselves' may still lead to 'the transmission of different cultural heritages to Protestant and Catholic children.' In the area of history in particular Stewart (1977), a noted Northern Irish historian notes that because of the history that each child learns at his mother's knee as well as 'in school, in books and plays, on radio and television, in songs and ballads' each community 'identifies itself with the myth it takes from Irish history.' The importance of history teaching should not be ignored, particularly as it is considered by many to play a critical role in situations where ethnic identity has been maintained over many generations. Here 'history assumes an especial importance in ethnic identity formation. . . providing people with a perception of their past, enabling them through the selective stressing of certain values to make positive identifications with their forebears' (Epstein, 1978).

It must be remembered of course that everything that happens in schools is not under the direct control of teachers. Indeed, even everything that is taught in schools is not taught by teachers. A neglected question therefore, has been the possibility that schools in Northern Ireland may be passing on certain values to their children which help form the flames of conflict, but that this information may be passed not from teacher to child but from child to child. One attempt to examine this possibility was a study (Austin, 1986) which recorded the games, stories and rhymes used by children in the playgrounds of over one hundred primary schools, Catholic and Protestant, in Northern Ireland.

What this investigation revealed is that indeed the playground is a place where Northern Irish children learn not only to be boys and girls but also to be Protestants and Catholics. One example of the way in which the playground reinforces cultural identity, claims Austin (1986), is the fact that in Catholic schools children's rhymes are more likely to draw upon religion and history than are those in Protestant schools. Indeed, Austin suggests that in about 10 per cent of the schools studied, usually those in urban areas with a history of violent intergroup conflict, the rhymes used by *boys* included a 'strongly scatalogical element'. So much so that all were virtually unprintable. On a more subtle level he notes that the game 'British Bulldogs' played in Protestant schools becomes just plain 'Bulldogs' or even 'Irish Wolfhounds' in Catholic schools.

Divided Children?

In the end of course the proof of the pudding is in the eating and the final verdict must therefore depend not so much on comparisons involving the separate school systems but upon differences between the products of these two systems – the children of Northern Ireland. Unsubstantiated claims have in fact existed for some time that the schools in Northern Ireland do exert a definite pressure on the minds of their children.

Bernadette Devlin, one of the leading 'revolutionary' Catholic politicians of the early 1970s tells in her autobiography *The Price of My Soul* how her headmistress, a nun, conveyed to her pupils that 'everything English was bad.' Similarly McCann (1974), another politician of the same era describes how his history teacher 'was at pains to discredit English propaganda' and at the beginning of each school year would 'lead the class through the set text-book instructing them to tear out *passages of fiction*' (my italics). On the other hand these two teachers must have overseen the education of hundreds of Catholic children and launched many into the world who did not become Bernadette Devlins or Eamon McCanns – as a recent writer to the editor of the *Belfast Telegraph*, anxious to defend Catholic schools, was at some pains to point out. What had struck this person was the fact that Gerry Adams, head of Sinn Fein, the political wing of the IRA – and indeed alleged by many to have been himself at one time an active IRA man – was a former pupil of a school on Belfast's Falls Road called St Finian's Boys. Gerry Adams is of course a well-known public figure in

Northern Ireland (and possibly in Britain) and certainly something of a folk hero to many Catholic young people. But apparently he is not the first such folk hero that St Finian's Boys has produced. Its first was one James Magennis who as Seaman Magennis, Royal Navy, fighting for King if not for country, won the only Victoria Cross (Britain's highest award for valour) to come to Northern Ireland in the Second World War.

It could be argued that these two events were decades and even worlds apart. More broadly based contemporary evidence as to the possible impact Catholic and/or Protestant schools may have on their pupils comes from a study by McKernan (1980). McKernan, not without reason, hypothesised that there would be differences between Protestant and Catholic young peoples' value systems because of the operation of the so called 'Protestant ethic'. Further, he also hypothesised that the major difference between the two groups would be revealed more clearly by an examination of the way each felt their goals in life could be reached (instrumental values) rather than by comparing the actual goals themselves (terminal values). To test these hypotheses McKernan asked 751 fifteen-year-old school children from both denominations to complete the Rokeach value survey. This consists of eighteen terminal and eighteen instrumental values such as salvation and wisdom (terminal) and polite and clean (instrumental) which the children were asked to rank order.

The results obtained were quite the opposite to those which had been expected. To begin with, only two of the eighteen instrumental values revealed a statistically significant difference between the ranks awarded by the Catholic and Protestant subsamples. (This compared markedly to eleven out of eighteen differences when boys were compared with girls!) On the terminal values, however, six out of the eighteen were ranked differently by the two groups. Three of these were ranked more highly by Protestants – an exciting life, a world at peace, a world of beauty – while three were ranked more highly by Catholics – equality, freedom and self-respect. McKernan (1980) suggests that these differences are not related to the Protestant ethic as he had earlier suspected but rather to Northern Irish politico-religious differences. In particular he suggests that it is psychologically significant that the biggest differences between the two groups were reserved for the values equality and freedom. The Rokeach approach to measuring values is a fairly tried and trusted one. Nevertheless, as McKernan himself notes there are some serious questions which have to be raised about such research.

The most important of these is do the various value terms have exactly the same meaning for Catholics as for Protestants and in particular did both groups interpret the values equality and freedom in exactly the same way. It could also be argued that if they did not these results are all the more interesting, suggesting that two groups of young people inhabiting the same geographical area of the same small island and speaking the same language may still be living in different psychological worlds.

Evidence that this may indeed be so comes from another study which happily does not involve these conceptual problems. Robinson (1971) asked children in Derry, the second city of Northern Ireland, a series of straightforward questions such as 'Which country is Derry situated in?', 'What is the capital of this country?' etc. What the results of this study revealed was an almost complete dichotomy of answers from the two groups of children, Catholic and Protestant. As far as most Catholic children were concerned they lived in a country called Ireland whose capital was Dublin (that is the capital of the Irish Republic). Protestant children however replied that they lived in a country called Northern Ireland whose capital was Belfast. Derry is of course a divided city, one in which residential segregation is marked and where sectarian feelings have reached fever pitch from time to time. Indeed, there is a fundamental disagreement about the very name of the city – Derry according to most Catholics and Londonderry according to most Protestants. It is therefore important to note that at least one other study (Cairns and Duriez, 1976) has obtained a very similar result but this time in a relatively trouble-free, residentially integrated small town.

Perhaps the most alarming note in Robinson's study was the fact that the differences between the two groups became more apparent as the children got older. One might imagine that as children learned more about the world their views would become more similar. Certainly it could be hoped that those who survived the segregated educational system and eventually reached the apparent normality of one of the two integrated universities in Northern Ireland would show more signs that they were inhabiting the same psychological space as their peers across the denominational divide. This does not seem to be so however, judging by the results of a study by Boal and Orr (1978). These investigators, over a nine-year period (1969-77), charted the residential preferences of Catholic and Protestant first-year university students who were asked to select and rank their five most favourite and five least favourite regions in the British Isles. To help them do this the students were presented with an inverted map of the British Isles which had marked on it twenty-three different regions including two in Northern Ireland, four in the Republic of Ireland, five in Scotland with the remainder in England and Wales. An examination of the 'top' five and 'bottom' five regions revealed startling differences between those areas chosen by students who had attended Catholic schools and those who had attended Protestant schools. In the top five the south-west of England and the south coast of England were popular with both groups, while the southernmost region of Ireland plus the Dublin area figured in the Catholic students' list only. The rest of Northern Ireland (that is excluding Belfast) and the Edinburgh area appeared only in the Protestants' list however. More remarkable still, Boal and Orr were able to demonstrate that these preferences varied with time and in particular were apparently related to the rise and fall of the level of violence in Northern Ireland during the 1970s. Thus, for example, in 1972 when violence was at its height the Belfast area became less popular for both Catholic and Protestant young people. Similarly the Republic of Ireland as a whole became much more popular with Catholic students over the period 1971-77, while the Protestant students' preference for this area decreased.

Of course, as usual in reporting this sort of comparative study it is only too easy to make much of differences and ignore similarities. Nevertheless, as noted above, in many of the Catholic schools more stress is apparently placed on the history of Ireland and. indeed its general culture. Further, the games which are more frequently played, the Gaelic games, are played on an all-Ireland basis which may lead to greater contacts between Catholics in Northern Ireland and the Republic. Indeed, it is likely that a greater proportion of teachers in the Catholic schools are from the Republic especially those who are members of religious orders. What is significant about Boal and Orr's data, however, is that there is a suggestion that these differences may be dormant, to a certain extent, only coming to the fore at times when sectarian feelings are at their height.

A similar explanation could account for data gathered in two major surveys in Northern Ireland in the late 1960s and early 1970s. The first of these, the so called 'Loyalty Survey' (Rose, 1971), involved a random sample of over 1,000 Northern Irish adults in August 1968 while the second involved a non-random sample of over 3,000 schoolboys, those over eleven years of age being interviewed in early 1971 and those under eleven years in late 1971 and early 1972 (Russell, 1974). The dates here are of critical importance. In 1968 when Rose carried out his survey Northern Ireland had still to witness its first non-violent civil rights demonstration let alone experience death and destruction on its streets. In early 1971, when Russell began his fieldwork, deaths had now occurred, but it was only in the period between the end of this survey of the older (secondary) schoolboys and the beginning of the survey of primary schoolboys that an event occurred which, according to many, marked the watershed of political violence in Northern Ireland – the introduction of internment without trial in August 1971. In effect it is therefore possible to consider these surveys as a series each of which presents a snapshot of attitudes at three points in time, before the troubles began, during the build up to violence and when violence was at its height. Unfortunately this change in level of violence is 'confounded', to use the technical term, with a change in age of the respondants in that as the violence increased the age of the respondants decreased.

Despite this it is still tempting to compare the results from the three points in time. In particular it is interesting to note that each time the question was asked 'would you say people (in England/Republic of Ireland or of the opposite religion to you) are much different or about the same as you?' there was a tendency for Protestants to see themselves as increasingly more like the English and less like those in the Republic or Catholics in the north. In turn these changes were mirrored by changes in the opposite direction by Catholic respondants. For example, in Rose's study 66 per cent of Protestants in 1968 said they were different from the English but this fell to 43 per cent in 1971 and 35 per cent in late 1971 in Russell's survey (the corresponding figures for Catholics were 63 per cent, 58 per cent and 58 per cent). As far as attitudes towards people in the Republic were concerned for Protestants the figures were 46 per cent in 1968, 68 per cent in early 1971 and 71 per cent in late 1971 reporting that they were 'different', with the corresponding figures for Catholics being 48 per cent, 30 per cent and 35 per cent.

There are two possible explanations for these results. One is that as children become older and move away from the narrow confines of their separate school systems they realise that they are less like their alter-ego group in England (for the Protestants) or in the Republic (for the Catholics). If this were so there might be grounds to see this as evidence which could be used to condemn the segregated school system. At the same time it would suggest that the effects of those systems may not be as long lasting as some have feared.

An alternative explanation, however, is that these data mirror those obtained by Boal and Orr (1978) by suggesting that in times of heightened conflict, such as when the primary schoolboys survey was undertaken, certain attitudes are markedly sharpened. Clearly this is a question which will only be settled by further research with data gathered at all three age levels but at the same point in time. For the moment the 'increasing violence' explanation must be favoured however.

Yet the responses to the third part of the question posed by both Rose (1971) and Russell (1974) do not favour either explanation. This question basically asked 'Are you the same as or different from those on the other side of the religious divide in Northern Ireland?' In 1968 only 28 per cent of Protestants and 14 per cent of Catholics replied 'different'. By early 1971 these figures were now 45 per cent and 41 per cent and by late 1971 56 per cent and 47 per cent for Protestants and Catholics respectively. This information does however raise an other important issue in the debate about segregated education, and that is the question of intergroup contact. The argument over whether segregated schools influence the attitudes their pupils hold about the other side and about such nebulous issues as Irish and British culture is a difficult one to resolve empirically. For this reason the debate will no doubt flourish but largely at the level of rhetoric. What is not open to debate however is the fact that to some extent at least segregated schools necessarily reduce the amount of contact Catholic and Protestant children have with each other. The important question is, of course, how extensive is this separation in everyday life – that is outside school hours?

Fortunately, once again some pre-troubles baseline data are available in this area. For example, in an early survey of 361 adults Jenkins and MacRae (1966) recorded that about 30 per cent of their Catholic respondants and under 20 per cent of Protestants reported that half or more of their friends were from the opposite religious group. Comparable figures from the survey by Rose in 1968 are 42 per cent for Catholics and 19 per cent for Protestants. In other words, both these studies suggested that, before the troubles began, there were some personal friendships which reached across the religious divide. Moxon-Browne (1979) reported similar information from a survey of over one thousand adults in Northern Ireland in 1978 for both Catholics and Protestants combined. This reveals that while 30 per cent of the total numbers of respondants in 1968 reported that all of their friends were from the other community, this figure had fallen to 19 per cent in 1978 (Moxon-Browne, 1979). There is a suggestion here that it is personal relationships that were particularly influenced by the escalation in political violence in the period 1968-78 for during that time the numbers of neighbours and workmates *all* of the opposite religion remained constant at around 30 per cent and 19 per cent respectively.

Even in a small society such as Northern Ireland one number will not always do justice to the complexity of people's feelings and attitudes. Therefore, it is not surprising that Jenkins and MacRae noted that in their small survey they could still detect differences between people from different geographical locations. In particular, they suggested that the more closely in size the two communities resembled each other the less crossing of the denominational divide occurred. It seems in this respect that things may not have changed very much because Poole (1982) adopting a much more sophisticated approach and based on more broadly based data reports that levels of segregation in residential accommodation are indeed influenced by the size of the local minority group. Thus in any town where the local minority is large, be it Catholic or Protestant, the level of religious residential segregation is high. Overall therefore the picture of intergroup contact among adults is a complex one almost certainly influenced by such factors as the current level of sectarian feeling and more local factors such as local minority group size. The important point perhaps is that such contact does occur – although as the contact situation becomes more intimate the amount of contact decreases. Thus in what is perhaps the ultimate of intimate associations, marriage, intergroup contact is extremely limited with, according to Rose (1971), the numbers marrying across religious lines as small as 4 per cent.

Regrettably, the same level of information is not available where intergroup contact between children is concerned. Additionally there is the problem that the data which are available often take a different form from that involving adults. This is a problem that always bedevils survey research, researchers will word their questions in slightly different ways, which makes comparisons between surveys that much more difficult. For example, Russell (1974) in 1972 asked his primary and secondary schoolboys whether they had friends across the religious divide, while McWhirter and Gamble (1982) some ten years later simply asked their respondents, who were all primary schoolchildren, 'Do you know anyone who is a. . . ?' Russell reports that in response to his question 50 per cent of the primary group and 60 per cent of the secondary group replied positively. It might have been expected that McWhirter and Gamble's broader question would have elicited even more positive replies but this was not the case. On average about 50 per cent of the children claimed they did know someone from the other religious group but this rate showed wide variations according to area with 70 per cent replying positively in a relatively peaceful area with a Protestant majority, 56 per cent in a relatively peaceful area with a Catholic minority, and 23 per cent in an area of intense conflict.

The only other evidence in this area is somewhat tangential and comes from the research, described earlier (*see* Chapter 5), by Cairns (1980) which investigated children's ability to categorise first names on a denominational basis. To do this he asked children to try to remember as many names as possible from a list containing equal numbers of Catholic, Protestant and 'foreign' names. As well as analysing the way these names were grouped or clustered on recall Cairns also examined the sheer number of names recalled in each category by the Protestant and Catholic children taking part. What Cairns found to his surprise was that Protestant children recalled significantly more Protestant than Catholic or foreign names while Catholic children recalled more Catholic names than Protestant or foreign. Considering that both groups of children attended separate schools, but schools quite close to each other in the same city, what was really disturbing was that the Protestant children failed to recall more Catholic names than foreign names. If, as Cairns (1980) suggested, these results are due to familiarity – that is that the children tended to recall more names from that set of names they were most familiar with – then it would appear that these young Protestant children were no more familiar with Catholic first names in everyday use in their own city than they were with first names used in other countries. The city where these data were gathered is admittedly one where segregation is fairly complete and sectarian violence common and for these reasons it is perhaps not surprising that intergroup contact would appear to be minimal – at least at this age level.

Based on this limited amount of information it could be cautiously concluded that the same general principles outlined above which govern adult intergroup contact in Northern Ireland also apply where children are concerned. That is, that contact does occur but that it is probably limited by residential segregation and by the occurrence of overt conflict. On the face of it these are pretty unremarkable conclusions. There is, however, a further factor which is worth mentioning. There is, in the adult data in particular, the suggestion that Catholics are more likely to form social relationships across the religious divide. Why should this be so? One explanation which has been offered in the past is that in Northern Ireland Catholics are more 'open' than are Protestants. This is certainly a distinct possibility. A simpler explanation, however, is that on a probability basis alone it would be predicted that a Catholic is more likely to encounter a Protestant given that there are roughly twice as many Protestants as Catholics living in Northern Ireland. Certainly this could account for there being, in the data on names, approximately twice as many people with typically Protestant first names in Northern Ireland as there are people with typically Catholic first names.

Reaching across the Divide

One way to test this idea is to gather comparable data in situations where Catholic and Protestant children have an equal opportunity of meeting each other such as a school. Unfortunately, as noted earlier, such occasions are extremely rare in Northern Ireland. But this does not mean that they do not exist at all. Such is the nature of Northern Irish society however that these islands of integration in an ocean of segregation do not usually care to draw attention to their existence. No doubt this is the reason that only relatively recently have a few integrated schools been 'discovered' by researchers. Fortunately, now that they have been discovered some interesting findings are beginning to emerge.

According to McWhirter (1983b), who has reviewed this research, these integrated – or at least desegregated – schools fall into roughly three categories. First of all there are some grammar schools which are predominantly Protestant but are attended by some local Catholic children, often because a suitable Catholic school is not available within reasonable travelling distance. Secondly there are some primary schools which did not originate on a denominational basis in contrast to most primary level schools in Northern Ireland. Those schools were mostly established by nineteenth-century mill owners for the children of their workers. Because in some cases the workforce was 'mixed' in religious terms, today, although now officially government-run controlled schools, these schools still retain their integrated nature. Ironically however the majority of integrated schools are those which are labelled 'special schools' – not because they are integrated but because they cater specifically for children who are handicapped either physically or mentally. Writing in 1972 when sectarian violence was of course at its height Fraser notes that there were at that time some 1,500 children attending such schools, many bussed in from their respective ghettos. Just why these schools are not organised along religious lines is not clear. As McWhirter (1981) notes, it is a curious fact that, given the degree of interest the churches have shown in the remainder of the educational system they do not seem to have the same interest in Northern Ireland's special schools. In fact Fraser (1974) remarked that he was left with the shattering conclusion that these children 'must be thought to be too stupid to be corrupted by integration.'

The observations of those involved in these desegregated institutions in Northern Ireland suggest that on the whole they have been relatively successful. For example, Fraser, writing about special schools in an article with the rather emotive title, 'At School During Guerrilla War' notes that he was told, even in 1972, that there was no evidence of polarisation between Catholic and Protestant children within the schools. Blease (1983), the principal teacher in a special school for children with emotional problems, echoed this opinion some ten years later remarking that, taking into account the sectarian nature of the violence which surrounded the school, the teachers had always been surprised by the lack of religious conflict between the pupils. He does however admit that at certain times, for example during the hunger strike, tension might become more evident but that such rifts were not permanent. Similarly, Lockhart and Elliott (1980) remark that the teen-age boys they studied in the desegregated residential assessment centre at first tended to keep to their own religious groups but that these divisions disappeared within a space of two or three days when children would begin to make friends regardless of religion. What is particularly interesting about this centre is that it is a residential one where Protestant and Catholic boys live together for a period of some five weeks.

A more objective method of measuring friendship patterns is the technique known as sociometry. Basically in a sociometric study children, or indeed adults, are asked to nominate one or more other members of their group who they, for instance, like most or would like to work with most on some particular task. In a study involving over 400 children from special schools, ages ranging from three to nineteen years, McWhirter (1981) employed such a sociometric technique to measure actual and preferred choices within such categories as playmate, best friend etc. The results of this study revealed that in only four out of 280 analyses did the pattern of friendship choices within desegregated school classes differ from that expected by chance. McWhirter does note, however, that two slight trends appear in the results. The first was that older children's choices were more likely to differ from chance than were the choices of younger children and secondly that where choices differed from those expected by chance children of the same religion were usually involved in actual choices while children from the other religion were more likely to be involved in preferred choices. McWhirter does not offer any explanation for this pattern of results and it is difficult to know how they should be evaluated based as they are on fairly small numbers of classes each containing relatively small numbers of children.

Davies and Turner (1984) report the use of the same technique but this time with 100 children aged seven to eleven years in an integrated mill school. They asked children at four different age levels to make sociometric choices related to the classroom, play at school and play at home. Again, the results suggest that there is virtually no evidence of a religious barrier in the classroom or in play at school. However, where playmates away from school were concerned Protestant children consistently chose other Protestants more often than would have been expected by chance. Davies and Turner (1984) note that while this may be evidence of religious bias, it is more likely to simply represent residential segregation in the school's catchment area. Indeed, this may be a further example of the fact that simply on a probability basis Catholics are more likely to interact with Protestants than vice versa.

Of course, one of the problems about this research technique is that it does not make clear whether children are choosing their friends and playmates from members of the other religious group with a consciousness that they were indeed of 'the other sort'. Instead these results may simply indicate that children in desegregated school settings are not aware that other children in their class are not of the same religion as themselves. Some evidence to back up this idea comes from two further studies in desegregated school settings. In the first of these Gamble (1982) found that few children in a desegregated school were actually aware of the 'mixed' nature of the school they were attending. Lawless (1981) compared a group of children attending 'normal' segregated schools with a small number (37) of handicapped children who were pupils at desegregated special schools. The results from this study are particularly interesting in that when the children were asked if they knew any Protestants and any Catholics no significant differences emerged between the children from the desegregated and segregated schools. In other words, contrary to what might have been expected more children from the desegregated schools did not report that they knew children from the opposing group.

This could be an important result because critics of the idea of integrated education have always hinted, as Akenson (1973) puts it, that 'integration can also increase social tensions and worsen groups relations.' The suggestion in the study by Lawless (1981) that it does not do so is therefore particularly comforting especially as it reinforces a similar view put forward earlier by Cairns (1980). Based on a study in a desegregated mill school he had noted that there was no evidence that children there were more likely to be able to categorise first names on a denominational basis than children in segregated schools.

The general impression, therefore, is that desegregated schools in Northern Ireland may be helping to form friendships which cut across the religious divide even though these friendships may have difficulty in flourishing outside school hours. In addition there is no evidence that desegregated schools are in any way heightening children's awareness of the division within Northern Irish society. All of this is particularly welcome given the movement that is gathering momentum to develop purpose-built desegregated schools in Northern Ireland. This began with a group of parents, dissatisfied with the conventional arrangements, who formed themselves into an association known as All Children Together. In 1981 in Belfast a breakaway movement from this group opened the first secondary school in Northern Ireland whose avowed aim is to cater for children from both communities – Lagan College. Following this pioneering effort by 1986 five such schools were in operation, four in the Belfast area and one in South Down, three at the primary level and two at the secondary level. To date these schools appear to be having little problem in recruiting pupils. Yet while the movement is growing in popularity it must be recognised that such schools are catering for but a fraction of the school population of Northern Ireland. Nevertheless this is at least, in the eyes of their founders, a beginning.

Ironically, at the same time as these would-be healing processes are underway in the school system other more divisive forces are also at work. For example, recently one of the more fundamental Protestant sects has taken steps to open its own church-run primary schools paralleling on the Protestant side the voluntary schools of the Catholic educational sector. A further recent development which may also widen the gap in education is a controversy which has broken out in the western educational area of Northern Ireland. This is a predominantly Catholic area and as a result Catholics are in the majority and therefore control power where local political matters are concerned. What has recently incensed Protestants in this area however is that Catholics are beginning to dominate the committees, and especially their chairmanship, which run the state sector of education in this part of Northern Ireland. Through Protestant eyes this means that the Catholics while retaining their own Catholic school system also wish to control the *de facto* Protestant or state schools. Any legal move of course to recognise the Protestants' grievance would endanger the *de jure* status of the state schools as non-denominational and could thus lead to recognition of their *de facto* denominational status.

To this list of potentially divisive forces in education must be added the establishment of Bunscoil Gaeilge – the primary school in west Belfast where all teaching is via the medium of Irish. This school's popularity has increased markedly over the last five years in particular, the school's numbers having risen from 7 in 1971 to 97 in 1982 and 152 in 1984. An outgrowth of this school's success has been the establishment of linked nursery schools (Maiscoil) of which there are now at least four in Belfast. Were this movement to develop outside west Belfast and to extend into the secondary school system, its influence could extend well beyond the Catholic community it would initially affect. As noted earlier although Irish has traditionally been taught in Catholic schools it has not been particularly successful. This no doubt is because it has been taught largely as a 'foreign' language and in a fairly academic way. The result is that the teaching of Irish in the Catholic school system has produced relatively few fluent speakers of the language. However, this new movement may revolutionise all this and could in time produce a new generation of Northern Irish Catholics who actually can and do speak Irish. The fact that linguistic rights of minorities are guaranteed by the United Nations and by the European Convention on Human Rights plus the fact that virtually no Protestants learn Irish means that this movement could produce, within one or two generations, a major social change in Northern Ireland whose ramifications could extend well beyond narrow educational concerns and end perhaps forever the dream of integrated education in Northern Ireland.

Conclusions

As places where Northern Ireland's children learn the three 'Rs' the schools of Northern Ireland must be considered to be relatively successful institutions. Indeed, it is probably true to say that there is a certain amount of smug satisfaction in Northern Ireland that the rather traditional educational system favoured by both sides of the community has often out-performed more trendy systems in other parts of the United Kingdom. However, school is not only a place where children learn to read and write but is also a primary socialisation agent in any society. In this role there is less agreement about how successful Northern Ireland's schools have been. Indeed, some would claim that they have failed dramatically.

The evidence for this, critics would assert comes from the fact that Catholic children apparently see themselves as Irish, living in a temporarily detached part of an otherwise free and Republican Ireland while Protestant children largely see themselves as British and living in 'what is after all just another part of the United Kingdom.' Empirical evidence to pin the blame for this state of affairs on the divided school system however is clearly missing. Indeed, the few investigations that have made comparisons across the two school systems have been surprised by the similarities they have found rather than the differences. Despite this lack of evidence commentators continue to see the divided school system as a major cause of the conflict in Northern Ireland. For example, in a politically oriented book Boyle and Hadden (1985) in their chapter entitled 'Northern Ireland: Why it Failed' boldly assert that 'the process of segregation begins with education.'

Clearly, this is an area where much more research is needed. Research which would if possible disentangle for example the effect of family, peer group and schooling on socialisation in Northern Ireland. For the moment however the verdict in the case against the schools must remain one of 'not proven'. There are of course those who have suggested that integrating the schools far from reducing friction would actually increase it. It is therefore comforting to note that what little evidence is available suggests that this would not be the case and that Catholic and Protestant children can exist happily side by side – at least in the classroom. It is also comforting to note that while the majority of schoolchildren in Northern Ireland attend segregated schools there are some children who attend desegregated schools even if these schools are desegregated by accident rather than by design and an even smaller number who attend schools which have been designed to be integrated from the moment of their inception. Happily this latter trend appears to be growing albeit slowly. More worrying however is the trend in the opposite direction, that is for certain sections on the fringes of both communities to set up their own separate schools. This combined with the evidence which suggests that friendships which cross the sectarian divide have been dwindling since the onset of the troubles points to the conclusion that there is now an urgent need for social scientists and educationalists concerned with resolving conflict to encourage the infant integrated school movement and where possible to provide advice to help ensure that its future is a successful one. In the end one must agree with Akenson (1983) that while it is '*probable* but by no means proved that the segregated school system exacerbates intergroup frictions. . . it is *highly probable* that the segregated schools do nothing to neutralise hostile and prejudical attitudes between religious groups' (p. 200). In future therefore energy should be devoted not to debating whether segregation begins with schools in Northern Ireland but rather to attempting to ensure that it ends there, although, as the next chapter will demonstrate this need not mean – indeed perhaps should not mean – that all schools must be desegregated overnight. More subtle and more effective solutions may be available.

7

Politics and the Next Generation

Social scientists who venture abroad from Northern Ireland often find that a popular question in the minds of interested onlookers to the conflict is – 'How will it all end?' In crude terms there are three possible answers to such a question. First, it is possible that in general terms nothing will change and that the conflict will simply drone on forever as it has apparently always done. A blacker picture is to suggest that escalation will occur. That is, that the violence will increase in severity leading perhaps to a victory by one side or the other or, more likely, to 'a doomsday situation' similar perhaps to the Lebanon in the 1980s. Finally there is the optimistic view that the two sides will get together eventually, suggesting that one day peace will return.

In a series of studies in South Africa (Du Preez *et al.*, 1981) outcomes somewhat similar to these were used to form a questionnaire measuring young people's expectations of the future. In this questionnaire five possible outcomes were posed: two of these, the 'conservative' and the 'technicist' corresponded roughly to the no change option noted above. Two others, 'catastrophe' and 'revolution' mirrored the escalation option while a fifth 'liberal' involved the prediction of a peaceful future fifty years from now. This research is of particular interest here because McWhirter (1983) asked a group of 234 well educated Northern Irish, sixteen to eighteen-year-olds (mostly girls – 70 per cent) to predict the probability that these particular futures were what awaited Northern Ireland fifty years from now. In this chapter the young people's predictions will be considered in turn and an evaluation will be made of the evidence relating to each in a Northern Irish context.

According to the questionnaire, the conservative future, as its name implies, involves a prediction that though the pattern of society may be temporarily disturbed things will remain very much as they are at present, while the technicist future predicted change would be technological and material only. In other words, both these options,

144

in Northern Irish political terms, represent the stalemate answer noted above. Perhaps not surprisingly, given the long history of the conflict in Northern Ireland the young people from there suggested that indeed these were the two most likely futures facing Northern Ireland fifty years from now ranking them one and two respectively. It is indeed this option that would appear to receive the biggest support from an orthodox view of political socialisation. A basic premise in the political socialisation literature has been, at least until recently, that 'the origins of the impetus to political involvement lie in the formative years of childhood' (Barner-Berry and Rosenwein, 1985). In other words, the received wisdom is that how adults will behave politically and the political attitudes they hold have been determined largely by socialisation processes which stretch back well into childhood and adolescence.

Early research in this area laid the blame squarely and fairly for this state of affairs on the shoulders of parents suggesting that 'early family socialisation' is 'one of the most important factors' in the political socialisation process (Almond, 1960). The suggestion that the source of party identification is the family was based on evidence (Greenstein, 1969) which suggests that, although they may not use explicit teaching, parents nevertheless are a prime source of information in this area. It has been suggested, for example, that children may overhear parental conversations or may be informally told of their parents' stance towards political matters in general and partisan politics in particular. Further, it is not unlikely that parents are called upon to answer questions about politics from time to time just as they are required to answer questions about a million and one other aspects of the society the child is growing up in (Greenstein, 1969).

Eventually, however, experts in this field began to question the role of the parents as the sole transmitters of political knowledge and attitudes and to their list added peers, school and the mass media as the principal agents of political socialisation. The family's role in establishing party affiliation was however still considered to be dominant.

Actually whether one accepts that the family is the most important of the agents of political socialisation is relatively unimportant in a divided society such as Northern Ireland. This is because, with segregation in schools and in social life and to some extent even in the media (newspapers in Northern Ireland are often partisan) the child's family, his or her friends and the school he or she attends are all likely to be providing a similar political message. This in turn would lead to the conclusion that in Northern Ireland the whole political socialisation process is one which is geared towards creating a resistance towards political change in any form. Certainly it would appear that such a set-up is at the very least likely to maintain the existing divisions and in turn to keep alive the potential for conflict if not the conflict itself.

Therefore, to paraphrase Greenstein (1969), all this would suggest that generations of voters coming of age in the year 2000 in Northern Ireland might be expected faithfully to reproduce voting patterns which have their roots in the experience of earlier generations in the violence of the 1970s. Hard evidence on this issue is however virtually non-existent but this is a state of affairs which many commentators have assumed exists. For example, Stewart (1977) notes that people in Northern Ireland 'simply assume the political attitudes of the faith into which they were born. They rarely choose their political outlook after mature deliberation.' Similarly O'Donnell (1977) studying mutual stereotypes in Northern Ireland concluded that the source of these stereotypes lay in traditional attitudes 'passed on by parents to their children for generations.'

In this respect it is interesting to note that in his 1968 survey Rose (1971) found that only 7 per cent of his (adult) participants could not recall whether, during their childhood, their parents thought of themselves as British, Ulster or Irish and only 4 per cent could not recall their parents' attitudes towards Protestants and Catholics mixing socially. Also there is evidence that at least one aspect of political behaviour in Northern Ireland has remained unchanged for some time. This is the proportion of the population who turn out to vote in elections both for the local assembly and for the Westminister parliament in London. Despite the fact that such elections have been quite numerous over the last fifteen years – an average almost of one election per year – normally 60 per cent or more of the population turn out to vote and in some constituencies this figure has reached 85 per cent and more. These figures compare favourably with an average of just over 50 per cent in presidential elections and around 35 per cent in elections for the House of Representatives. The fact that the numbers turning out to vote are being maintained or if anything are increasing suggests that new voters coming of age in the 1970s and 1980s are retaining this pattern of behaviour. Indeed a recent survey (IYB, 1985) of almost one thousand young people (aged sixteen to twenty-five years) indicated that of those old enough to vote 59 per cent claimed that they had already done so.

All of this paints a picture of a society in which the young, far from rebelling against the adult world, rather 'tend towards conformity with their parents and the local community' (Jenvey, 1972). In some parts of the world this might be received as good news, but given the past history of Northern Ireland this may herald a gloomy future for politics in this part of the world, suggesting at best that the conflict will continue in a steady state *ad infinitum*, thus continuing to dominate Northern Irish politics as it has done for at least the last fifty years.

Escalation

However, while it is true to say that the conflict has been in existence for this period of time it is not correct to say that nothing has changed in Northern Irish politics in the last fifty years. The biggest change of all has been the development of the conflict into almost continuous violence beginning in the late 1960s. What is most remarkable about this is the fact that the leaders of the Catholic community who were most involved in politics at this time were almost all young people who had grown up in the relatively peaceful atmosphere of Northern Ireland in the 1940s and 1950s. Taking this evidence into account could well mean that the best prediction for the political future in Northern Ireland is not simply a prolongation of the conflict at its present level but rather that the violence will escalate still further eventually reaching catastrophic proportions. This is the future that the young people in McWhirter's (1983) study thought was the next most probable after the two equally probable versions of a future involving no change. This means that some 60 per cent believed that there was a 50-50 chance or better that in the next fifty years in Northern Ireland things will go from bad to worse with little prospect of recovery from the present deadlock. Incidentally, fewer (42 per cent) saw a revolutionary outcome, with its implications of a new social order brought about by violence, as a 50-50 chance or better.

It would appear that whether one accepts this prognosis for politics in Northern Ireland depends not so much on any agreement about whether the conflict will continue; rather the question is how the next generations will attempt to seek to resolve their conflict – via the bullet or the ballot box? The fact, noted above, that the vast proportion of the Northern Irish population appear to be willing to turn out to vote in election after election might give some comfort and indeed lead to the conclusion that the people of Northern Ireland are committed to conventional politics. Whether this is true or not is difficult to assess.

Certainly the suspicion is that in Northern Ireland at any rate too much stress should not be laid on voting behaviour as an indicator of a belief in politics or the efficacy of orthodox political behaviour. As Rose (1971) has pointed out, in Northern Ireland voting is not seen so much as political behaviour but rather 'as a duty or as a means of expressing substantive loyalties.'

Therefore, the possibility exists that young people in Northern Ireland as they enter the political arena in the coming years will reject conventional politics as a solution to the conflict and instead will adopt more radical approaches particularly the use of violence. Certainly this is what Fields suspected was happening as early as 1973. As she put it 'violence and terrorism do not politicise young children, they turn instead to taking violent action – not toward political measures' (Fields, 1973). There is indeed some evidence from Northern Ireland and elsewhere to back up this suggestion. For example, in a study designed to understand how American culture came to be one which approves of violence, Owens and Strauss (1975) reanalysed data from a national survey of the USA carried out in 1968 which involved over one thousand adults. What they found was that approval of political violence as an adult was associated with violence experienced either directly or indirectly in childhood. Their conclusion therefore was that exposure to interpersonal violence can and does provide a model for acts of political violence.

This result fits well with one of the major psychological concepts used to explain how children learn to behave aggressively – the theory of modelling (Bandura and Walters, 1963). This theory, backed up by numerous impressive studies, suggests that children can acquire new behaviours simply by observing such behaviour in others. Further, this type of learning, research has suggested, is more likely to be effective when the model is reinforced or rewarded for his or her behaviour.

This is important because many would argue that those who advocate and indeed resort to violence for political reasons in Northern Ireland have indeed been rewarded in various subtle yet definite ways over the last fifteen years in particular. A further important finding in this research has been that children who observe a model and thus learn a new piece of behaviour may simply add this new behaviour to their behavioural repertoire of potentially employable behaviours without necessarily acting out that behaviour at the time the learning actually occurred. This means that the children who are undoubtedly learning about violence in Northern Ireland, as demonstrated in Chapter 2, may not be turning into *children* who indulge in aggressive behaviour but they could later turn into *adults* who either approve of or even use violence in a political context. In other words, the violence of the 1970s and 1980s could be providing a learning situation which will furnish the script for political behaviour in Northern Ireland over the next fifty years.

And there is some evidence, admittedly patchy, which appears to confirm that such a process may be underway in Northern Ireland. For example, in a series of studies Mercer and his colleagues (Mercer, 1980) claimed that they had data which indicated that a positive attitude towards violent change was more likely to be characteristic of those who had participated in the civil disturbances of the 1970s. This observation in turn echoes that made earlier by Russell (1974) who had noted that among his schoolboy sample approval of street disorder was associated this time with simply living in or near a riot-zone or reporting that your neighbourhood was one which had experienced 'some' or 'a lot' of trouble. Similarly more recently McWhirter (1983) in her study of young people's visions of the future in Northern Ireland found that 'those subjects who had had the greatest contact with violence valued revolution much more highly'.

Perhaps the most frightening aspect of all this is, as Mercer (1980) has pointed out, that once involved in violence young people may in effect find themselves locked into this form of political behaviour. This is because, he suggests, the processes involved may take the form of a type of 'self-perpetuating positive feedback loop' (Mercer and Bunting, 1980) where paradoxically questions about which factors constitute causes and which effects become almost meaningless. For example, one characteristic Mercer (1980) observed in adolescent demonstrators was that they were more likely to report feelings of being harrassed and threatened. Was this due to the fact that they had taken part in political demonstrations (i.e. a consequence) or was this the factor which caused them to demonstrate in the first place?

The late Jeanne Knutson, an expert in political psychology, was in no doubt that the feelings of threat come first and act as a spur to later violent political behaviour. Knutson (1981) in her theory of victimisation suggested that, normally, being the victim of violence – particularly state violence – leads to a passive acceptance of this state of affairs plus depression and the classic 'slave mentality'. However, under certain circumstances victimisation can bring about the realisation that such experiences are preventable but only via continued activity in defence of oneself. In effect the victim comes to realise, she suggested, that the potential penalties for violence are now less threatening than the certain results of passivity (Barner-Berry and Rosenwein, 1985). Knutson based this claim on information gathered during interviews with political activists all over the world. One interview which she quotes from at length in her article was with a young man in Northern Ireland, an active member of the IRA. This young man (she refers to him simply as 'Eamon') tells how despite coming from a traditional Republican background and knowing about the early events of the troubles he had not felt directly or personally involved until he and his family were evicted from their home which was then petrol bombed and burnt to the ground. His major memory of this event he told Knutson was 'the terror, the fear, physical fear.' From that day onwards he realised that the only way to overcome his fear that it would happen again was to go on the offensive; that his 'best means of defence was to attack' (Knutson, 1981). Such experiences have not been confined to just one side in the conflict, of course, and there must now be a considerable number of young people in Northern Ireland who have experienced victimisation either physically or psychologically during the last fifteen years. Yet it must be clearly understood that such young people still constitute only a fraction of all the young people of Northern Ireland whose formative years have paralleled those of the troubles. Nevertheless this is not a reason to be complacent because the reality of the situation is that urban guerrilla movements in the late twentieth century are by no means mass movements but rather rely on a small but dedicated band of believers. Therefore, if the number of young people experiencing victimisation in each year were only to be added to in terms of tens rather than tens of thousands this would probably be enough to guarantee that violence as a political option would grow in popularity.

Some political observers might argue that there is indeed evidence that this process is already underway. In this context many would point to the growing support for a relatively new political party in the nationalist/republican camp – Sinn Fein. Sinn Fein is in effect the political wing of the IRA and thus openly supports the 'armed struggle'. Although they did not run in the 1979 election they polled 10 per cent of the total vote in 1982 and increased this to 13.4 per cent in the 1983 election. If one assumes that the overwhelming majority of this support came from the Catholic community (a fairly safe assumption) then this means that by 1983 Sinn Fein was the party of choice for some 40 per cent of those in Northern Ireland who are against the union with Britain (Cox, 1984). What is interesting about this development is that many commentators believe that Sinn Fein has grown not simply by wooing voters from the moderate nationalist party the Social Democratic and Labour Party (SDLP) but to a much greater degree through the mobilisation of a 'new vote'. Further, according to many political observers this means not only adults who have never bothered to vote before or indeed abstained for political reasons, but particularly young people coming on to the electoral role for the first time. That said, it does help to put Sinn Fein's position into perspective by noting that the revolutionary future was considered to be the least unlikely to occur in the next fifty years by the young people in McWhirter's (1983) study. On the other hand it should be noted that most of them were female and presumably middle-class and Sinn Fein's support is predominantly working-class.

Political Interest: Up or Down?

It would appear therefore that there is evidence to suggest that children and young people in Northern Ireland are being politically socialised in such a way that will guarantee the continuation of the conflict or, worse still, lead to escalation.

It may be surprising therefore to learn that some social scientists are on record as suggesting that far from being interested or involved in the politics of conflict young people in Northern Ireland have actually become uninterested in and even downright bored with local politics in any shape or form.

For example, Ungoed-Thomas (1972) is on record as stating that 'the stereotype of adolescents being closely and personally involved in religious conflict' is one which 'goes against both common sense' and the evidence from his own research. In support of this position comes evidence from a study by Trew (1981a) in which she asked a group of Belfast university students the question 'who are you?' In their responses only 6 per cent of the students referred to politics and what is more, of that 6 per cent nearly half specifically mentioned their *lack* of involvement in politics.

The major problem in evaluating research such as that of Trew's is, however, the absence of comparable evidence either from other Northern Irish young people before the troubles began or from similar young people who are not Northern Irish. Fortunately several studies have now been carried out in which comparable data are available. The largest of these was the study which compared nine-, twelve- and fifteen-year-old boys and girls who lived in Northern Ireland, the Republic of Ireland, Jordan and Iraq – a total of 2,785 children (Hosin and Cairns, 1984). All of these children were given ten minutes to write an essay entitled 'My country' and these essays were then classified in terms of six categories including politics. In other words, a count was made of the number of children at each age level in each country who made any sort of reference to politics – for example to political figures or political institutions. What this revealed was that more children from the two Middle Eastern countries mentioned politics compared to both groups of Irish children. More particularly at every age level more children from the Republic of Ireland mentioned politics in the essays compared to Northern Irish children (overall a difference of 43 per cent compared to 28 per cent).

One possible interpretation of these results therefore is that (Cairns, 1983c) 'children in Northern Ireland over the age range nine to fifteen years show a markedly depressed level of political interest.' Of course, one has to be careful here because this interpretation depends very much on what exactly 'political' is taken to mean.

Nevertheless if one accepts Cairns' (1983c) interpretation of these results then they seem to be rather at odds with the conclusion reached by Whyte (1983) on the basis of her study of a small group of 91 Catholic children aged eleven and twelve years in west Belfast. Among these children Whyte claimed there was 'a lively interest in political matters.' She reached this conclusion on the basis of the children's ability to answer questions involving such things as the naming of three political parties, the meaning of the letters MP and their knowledge of the names of the Prime Minister of the United Kingdom and of the Republic of Ireland, the name of the Secretary of State for Northern Ireland and of the President of the USA. Whyte (1983) was pleasantly surprised at the relatively high level of knowledge of these children concerning matters political. However, what was particularly revealing was that the children performed best on questions relating to politics *outside* Northern Ireland. For example, 87 per cent were able to name the President of the USA but only 38 per cent could name the Secretary of State for Northern Ireland and only 34 per cent the Prime Minister of the Republic of Ireland. Whyte (1983) therefore concluded that in fact her results reveal that these children are simply echoing the attitudes of adults in Northern Ireland who perhaps 'have become apathetic through years of political frustration at a local level.'

In turn this observation of Whyte's may help to explain some other evidence which also appears to challenge Hosin and Cairns' (1985) conclusion that Northern Irish children and young people have no interest in politics. In 1985 a survey carried out involving 940 young people (sixteen to twenty-five-year-olds) found that 17 per cent reported that they were 'very' interested in politics. What is remarkable about this result is that in a survey in 1982 involving nearly 4,000 young people (fifteen to twenty-four-year-olds) in different European countries, 19 per cent had reported that they were 'really' interested in national politics. This would seem to suggest that about the same number of young people, adolescents and young adults in Northern Ireland are interested in politics as in other European countries. However, Whyte's (1983) observations now cast some doubt on this conclusion, suggesting instead that young people in Northern Ireland may be interested in politics but not necessarily in Northern Irish politics. Certainly any future research in this area will have to make clear exactly which political arena is being referred to.

An optimistic appraisal of these bits of information gleaned from various research studies might therefore suggest that indeed children and young people in Northern Ireland have become bored, uninterested, even disenchanted with local politics and have therefore also lost interest in the conflict *per se*. Unfortunately the fact that young people may no longer be interested in conventional politics does not necessarily mean that they are no longer committed to conflict. Indeed, one of the worrying aspects of Hosin and Cairns' (1985) results was that while fewer children from Northern Ireland mentioned politics more mentioned violence compared to the children from the other three countries. In fact the researchers hint at a possible inverse relationship (at least at a 'country' level) between mentions of violence and mentions of politics. Also, as noted earlier, for the conflict to be pursued through violent means the mass of the people do not have to be committed to the use of violence. Only a small group of dedicated individuals are needed to continue the violence at its present level. Therefore, even if the vast majority of young people have lost interest in local (Northern Irish) politics this does not necessarily guarantee an end to the conflict. It could in fact be argued that this political apathy on the part of the majority of young people carried into adulthood could leave the way open for the politics of violence to dominate in Northern Ireland in the years to come.

This assumption is based on the premise made in many western democracies that the silent majority represent what is often referred to as the 'centre'. As Utley (1975) points out, 'this is deemed to consist of the vast majority of mankind whose specific characteristics are held to be silence, moderation and a taste for compromise.' It is of course highly debatable whether the centre, in Northern Ireland, is indeed occupied by the majority of Northern Irish voters. Nevertheless it is paradoxically the very smallness of this group which makes it so important, because its leavening influence is so badly needed in Northern Irish society. It is therefore a group, many would argue, whose aspirations should be encouraged wherever possible. In Northern Irish politics the centre is occupied by one mainstream political party only – the Alliance Party. It has never managed to attract more than about 12 per cent of the vote and if anything its fortunes appear to be waning in the mid 1980s. There may be several reasons for this, for example the Alliance Party may be failing to motivate the traditionally apolitical centre or indeed it may be losing support to other more extreme parties. Those may be recoverable errors. However, another reason for the lack of viable centrist politics in Northern Ireland may be that the very people one would expect to occupy the political middle ground are voting with their feet and leaving Northern Ireland for good.

Emigration is not a new phenomenon in Northern Ireland. Like many other topics touched on in this book it is something Northern Irish people have learned to live with and almost every family can claim a relative in the USA or Canada or in Australia or New Zealand. However, by the late sixties emigration was becoming less common due both to an increasing standard of living in Northern Ireland and the decreasing need in the USA and elsewhere for new intakes of population.

According to newspaper reports at least, the onset of the conflict changed all that and in the early 1970s rumours were rife that, for example, three times as many people applied to go to Australia in 1971 as had done in 1967. Hard data were still difficult to come by but what little evidence there was suggested that those leaving were usually under forty and were either professionals or skilled workers. As it has often been suggested that the vast majority of those supporting the centre party in Northern Ireland are the better educated, more middle-class younger voters then this certainly suggests that if such emigration has indeed been occurring this may have affected the Alliance Party more than, for example, those parties at the extremes of the Northern Irish political continuum.

Some evidence to back up this assertion came in an early study by Russell (1974) which suggested first that about 40 per cent of the secondary school boys and 30 per cent of the elementary school boys questioned wanted to leave Northern Ireland when they were older and second that there were indications that 'the most peaceful boys desired most to escape the disorder.' Firmer evidence is now available to support these suspicions (Terchek, 1984). In a paper entitled 'Options to Stress: Emigration and Militancy in Northern Ireland' he claims that net emigration, which had reached its lowest annual rate for the century in the years prior to the outbreak of the conflict, had by 1975 doubled compared to its 1968 level. Certainly the 1981 census provides data which suggest that between 1971 and 1981 about 13,000 people per year left Northern Ireland in comparison to about 9,000 per year in the period 1951-61 and 6,000 per year in the period 1961-71.

Further, there is now also hard evidence that emigration has become a relatively popular option among the better educated of Northern Ireland's young people. For example, in a study encompassing all Northern Irish young people who entered university in 1973 and in 1979 (Osborne *et al.*, 1983) it was shown that those who opted to attend a university outside Northern Ireland had on average higher mean scores in their 'A' level examinations (while still at school) than those who remained to attend one of Northern Ireland's own universities. Of more interest here is the fact that when the 1973 cohort was followed up in 1980, of those who had left Northern Ireland in 1973 to study elsewhere the majority (63 per cent) were *still* living outside Northern Ireland. What all of this suggests is that every single year Northern Ireland is losing approximately 40 per cent of its brightest and most able young people and further that the majority of these are lost forever. Therefore, as Williamson *et al.* (1982) concluded there would appear to be evidence for 'a sizeable brain drain'. Interestingly this brain drain initially hits both sides of the religious divide about equally. However, Protestants are less likely to return to Northern Ireland once their studies are completed.

There is of course no clear evidence that the young people who emigrate are any more tolerant than those who live all their lives in Northern Ireland. However, Terchek (1984), in a reanalysis of data gathered by Rose in 1968, was able to find a trend which suggested that, for both Catholics and Protestants, those most likely to opt for emigration were on average less religious, more 'normatively integrated', and better educated. Overall, therefore the impression given to date by the limited information which is available suggests that a steady exodus of Northern Ireland's brightest (and probably most tolerant) young men and women is underway. As Williamson *et al.* (1982) have noted, it is likely that this will have 'a cumulative and undesirable effect on many aspects of economic, cultural and social life in Northern Ireland.' To this list might also be added political life, because as Terchek (1984) has pointed out, this exodus almost certainly means that Northern Ireland is being deprived of a moderating influence many would argue it badly needs. In other words, this emigration may be ensuring that slowly but surely Northern Ireland is becoming an even more divided society, with those remaining 'strong in their ethnic and political commitment' (Terchek, 1984).

Making Peace

None of this bodes well for the final scenario envisaged at the beginning of this chapter, that 'the two sides will get together eventually' and one day peace will return. In fact, given the evidence noted so far it is not surprising to learn that the young people asked to consider the possibility of a peaceful future for Northern Ireland fifty years from now predicted that this was the least likely outcome of all (McWhirter, 1983). To set against this however, there is the fact that while these young people considered peace the least likely development in the Northern Ireland of the future, they considered it by a long way the most desirable.

The question must therefore be asked, what can be done to increase the possibility that a peaceful future could become a more realistic prediction? Perhaps the one thing that people desirous of such a future in Northern Ireland have learnt over the last fifteen years is that the answer to this question is not to sit around waiting for peace to happen. It is not enough simply to give peace a chance, something more positive is required in the form of at least a gentle push if not a vigorous shove. I am glad to be able to report that already modest efforts are underway in this area.

These peacemaking efforts are of particular interest in the context of this book because they focus almost exclusively on children and young people. McCartney (1985) has questioned the reasons for this suggesting that perhaps young people are the targets of peacemaking activities simply because they are readily accessed for example in schools. However, there would seem to be other, better reasons why such schemes should concentrate on this particular age group. To begin with there is the, perhaps erroneous, assumption that 'you can't teach an old dog new tricks.' In other words, that it is more difficult to change adults' attitudes than it is to develop new attitudes in younger people. Then, if one takes the long term view there is no doubt that the children of today are the adults of tomorrow and there may be something to be said for adopting a strategy which searches for a solution to the conflict in the future rather than at once.

And there is also some concrete (if limited) research evidence to reinforce the view that children and young people are indeed potential peacemakers. For example, several studies have noted that while children are often aware of the violence going on in their society they seldom appear to condone such activities and indeed often condemn it (McWhirter, 1982). A typical example of this sort of sentiment is the following, written by a fifteen-year-old boy:

> Northern Ireland is a real dump, but if the fighting stopped it would be a great place.

This, allied to the evidence noted above that young people when asked see peace as the most desirable future for Northern Ireland, would appear to give the lie to any suggestion that children in Northern Ireland are warmongers, if anything, in the essays they write and in conversation one detects a certain war-weariness. But does this mean they are willing to accept peace at any price? Almost certainly not. As noted in Chapter 5, group loyalty is an important feature of Northern Irish society and plays an important role in the way people think about themselves, including their self-esteem.

Nevertheless, it has been suggested that young people in Northern Ireland are more tolerant of 'the other side' than one might expect. For example, a large study of over 2,000 secondary age children reported that on average young people were 'open rather than mistrustful towards the other side' (Greer, 1982). Overall, therefore, the picture we get of young people in Northern Ireland appears to confirm the impression provided by McKernan's (1980) study of Northern Irish young people's values. This suggested that the ideal for most children – both Catholics and Protestants – is a *world at peace* where they are *free* and *happy* and that this is to be attained by *honesty, cleanliness* and *love*. As McKernan (1980) points out this is a very idealised picture of end states of existence and human actions. Nevertheless, as he also usefully reminds us:

it underlines the idealism of youth, which should not be ignored by teachers, curriculum developers and all others with an educational responsibility. (McKernan, 1980, 133.)

How then have adults in Northern Ireland gone about nurturing this 'idealism of youth' in an attempt to produce a more tolerant and peaceful society? Consciously or unconsciously most of the efforts in this area to date appear to be premised on what has come to be known as the 'contact hypothesis.' This (Amir, 1969) is the commonly held belief that:

> contact between people – the mere fact of interacting – is likely to change their beliefs and feelings towards each other. . . . If only one had the opportunity to communicate with the others and to appreciate their way of life, understanding and consequently a reduction in prejudice would follow. (Amir, 1969, 319.)

In Northern Ireland part of the unspoken philosophy behind such schemes, labelled variously as community relations projects or reconciliation schemes, has been the belief that firstly, the earlier contact occurs between Catholic and Protestant children the more effective it would be and, secondly, the greater the sheer amount of contact the more effective it is likely to be. Reasoning along these lines the integration of the existing separate school systems appears to be a logical and positive policy for those who desire to foster peace and harmony in Northern Ireland. However, as discussed earlier in Chapter 6 the integrated school movement appears at present at any rate to be able to cater for no more than a small minority of the province's children. Partly this has to do with the questions of loyalty and identity that lie behind the very existence of the separate school systems but there are also practical reasons. Integrating the schools completely would almost certainly mean the adoption of bussing – that is, transporting children in both directions daily from their segregated residential areas to schools where integration could actually take place. For financial reasons if no other it seems unlikely that such a policy would ever be adopted. Perhaps as a recognition that long-term contact in integrated schools is unlikely ever to be a reality – at least for the vast majority of children in Northern Ireland – many organisations in the peace business have accepted what they probably feel is the next best option; intensive but short-lived contact in the form of integrated holidays. These holiday schemes appear to vary tremendously but common to all is the aim of bringing together roughly equal numbers of Protestant and Catholic children outside their own local environment for a limited period of time (from two to four weeks). In practice this often means taking children to neutral ground such as Scotland, Holland or even the USA. These children either live in summer camps or sometimes are hosted by a local family for the duration of their stay. While on holiday the children may be free to behave as tourists or they may be subjected to a fairly structured programme involving such things as games, athletic activities, hiking, etc.

In many ways these holidays have a tremendous appeal to common sense. The idea of taking children, often from deprived backgrounds, outside Northern Ireland and thus permitting them to see how the rest of the 'normal' world lives and allowing them to do so while mixing with children from 'the other side', could on the face of it do nothing but good. One early criticism, however, was that contact was not maintained after the holiday had ended. Today therefore many of these schemes try to keep their children in contact with followups of various sorts at least during the following winter. More serious and less easily overcome criticisms are for example that even if the present holiday schemes were to be extended greatly they could still only cater for a very small number of young people per year. Related to this is the emphasis in many of these programmes on taking children outside Northern Ireland which in turn means that this is a very expensive way to foster contact and so is a limiting factor.

These are fairly superficial criticisms, however, compared to those which can be levelled at all attempts to create peace in Northern Ireland based on the contact hypothesis. The contact hypothesis has in fact been extensively evaluated by social scientists in other countries particularly the USA. What this research strongly suggests is that contact *per se* does not necessarily reduce intergroup prejudice and indeed on rare occasions may actually lead to an increase in tension and ill feeling. To back up this assertion, writers often point to the fact that in South Africa today, and in the southern United States of the past, there was any amount of contact between the groups and yet this in no way fostered friendly relations or mutual understanding. Social scientists have therefore become much more realistic over the last twenty-five years about the role of contact in the reduction of intergroup conflict. Also, with the realisation that contact of itself is not a panacea for changing prejudices or promoting better intergroup relations has come an increased emphasis on a search for those special conditions under which intergroup contact may achieve this end. Some of the conclusions coming from this work are that among the favourable conditions which help to reduce prejudice are:

— equal status contact between the members of the groups involved or contact between members of a majority group and *higher* status members of a minority group
— contact which requires intergroup co-operation
— contact which is of an intimate rather than of a casual nature
— contact that is pleasant or rewarding.

Of particular importance here, it has been argued (Brown and Turner, 1981) is the distinction between interpersonal and intergroup contact (*see* Chapter 5). As discussed earlier the conflict in Northern Ireland is almost certainly an intergroup phenomenon related to the importance of social identity in Northern Irish society. This in turn suggests that if reconciliation is to be achieved then contact should take place at an intergroup level and not simply at an interpersonal level. The problem with integrating schools or integrated holidays is that they do not necessarily guarantee that such intergroup contact will occur. Indeed, recent reports of an attempt to evaluate a number of such holiday schemes (McWhirter and Trew, 1985) suggest that if anything the emphasis may be rather more on interpersonal contact. For example, they note that on one particular holiday neither the children nor their parents were aware of the community relations aims of the holiday. In other words, they did not know that children from both sides of the community were taking part. Indeed, they go on to report than on one particular holiday in the USA 'after four weeks some of the ten-year-olds did not realise that their friends were not of the same religion as themselves' (McWhirter and Trew, 1985). Similarly on other holidays it was noted that the discussion of differences in politics or religion, while not exactly banned, was certainly not encouraged.

McCartney (1985) has provided an overview of the many forms of reconciliation projects underway at present which appears to confirm this suspicion that intergroup contact is the exception rather than the rule. As he puts it projects which can be categorised as 'facing the music' are relatively rare. That is, projects where contact *per se* is not considered to be sufficient but rather discussion and exploration of the issues which divide the two communities are entered into. Instead, he suggests the bulk of projects can be labelled as encouraging superficial contact only ('passing the time of day'); at best only interpersonal contact may be fostered, (the 'happy families' category) or, perhaps least satisfactory, contact may be secondary to some other issue or activity (the 'hidden agenda' category).

It should be stressed that this is not to suggest that these various schemes do no good at all. For a child who lives in the back streets of Belfast to have a holiday of any sort is undoubtedly good for that child. However, it must be stressed that the form of interpersonal contact fostered across the sectarian divide by such projects will at best produce a child who can honestly claim 'some of my best friends are Catholics/Protestants *BUT*. . . .' In other words, what the organisers of such schemes have failed to appreciate is that 'prejudice and discrimination between groups are likely to be reduced more effectively by policies addressed directly to changing people's social identifications and inter-group relations' (Brown and Turner, 1981).

One must not blame holiday scheme organisers too much in this respect however. The fact of the matter is that in supressing or failing to encourage open discussion of the conflict and its political and religious ramifications they are simply acknowledging a convention recognised by almost everyone in Northern Irish society. This convention which was alluded to in Chapter 1 is that politics and religion are avoided as topics of conversation when one is in 'mixed' company. As McFarlane (1979) a social anthropologist has noted, this convention appears to arise from a desire to avoid giving offence to the 'other side'. However, a more complex explanation has been suggested by Thompson (1983). He claims that in many plural societies, including Northern Ireland, there is in effect a wish to deny that a conflict actually exists.

Support for Thompson's idea may be seen in the way people in Northern Ireland have expected their education system to respond to the conflict. Here the main desire has been to preserve the schools as 'havens of peace' where children are sheltered from the troubles and the political situation is thus rarely if ever mentioned (Russell, 1973). Also it would appear that parents have not really changed their minds about the role schools should play in this respect. Thus a recent survey (*Belfast Telegraph*, November 1984) revealed that only 23 per cent of the respondants believed that teachers should allow their pupils to know their political beliefs. This the newspaper interpreted as revealing that most Northern Irish parents definitely want to keep politics out of schools.

Overcoming this denial syndrome is undoubtedly a major obstacle to promoting peace and reconciliation in Northern Ireland. Without a more open discussion of Northern Ireland's problems it seems unlikely that genuine intergroup contact will ever be possible, and without such contact the structure of intergroup relations seems unlikely to alter in the foreseeable future. One place to begin such discussions might in fact be in the schools – after all, as noted in Chapter 6, topics pertinent to the conflict are almost certainly already taught in schools, particularly in history and social science classes. An ideal system therefore might be one in which children discussed various aspects of the conflict within their own separate schools and then came together to continue these themes in discussion or simply further study with children from the opposing school system. In this way children would be equipped with the necessary background knowledge and any contact that would occur would be more likely to take place on an intergroup rather than an interpersonal basis. This is of course not a new idea; the possibility was raised by early pioneers in this area who have tried to promote the inclusion of topics related to the conflict in the school curriculum and also to encourage co-operation between the two school systems.

However, according to a report by Dunn *et al.* (1984) which examined the amount of contact between schools in three contrasting areas of Northern Ireland, co-operation between schools is, to say the least, limited. This research, which was based on semi-structured interviews with school principals and teachers, came to the conclusion however that the lack of co-operation between schools may be as much to do with the nature of schools as inward-looking, self-contained institutions as it has to do with the wider issue of community relations in a divided society. While this report therefore suggests that the early pioneering efforts to bring schools together may have had little impact there is a glimmer of hope on the horizon. This is because the government, in the shape of the Department of Education for Northern Ireland (DENI), is now apparently actively promoting this role for schools.

Acknowledgement of government approval for educational involvement in promoting reconciliation in Northern Ireland came first in the form of a circular to all schools which pointed out that schools had a responsibility to formulate and 'sponsor policies for the improvement of community relations' and to be involved in activities which would ensure that:

> children do not grow up in ignorance, fear or even hatred of those from whom they are educationally segregated. (DENI circular June 1982.)

Words alone are not enough, of course, and it is important that the government gives practical support to schools if they are to implement these ideas. In this respect it is encouraging to know that the Department of Education has set aside a budget of £300,000-400,000 to support initiatives in this area (though this is only a drop in the ocean compared to the millions of pounds that the conflict costs per year). Part of this practical support will come from a newly formed steering group on Education for Mutual Understanding which has been set up under the auspices of the Northern Ireland Council for Education Development. It will be part of the brief of this committee to help to decide how this money should be spent and to help promote curriculum development related to education for reconciliation.

While this gives some cause for hope, the magnitude of the task facing schools in this area should not be forgotten. To begin with as noted above society in general in Northern Ireland does not appear to favour open discussion of the conflict nor does it appear to favour such activities in its schools. Further, this work will undoubtedly touch on sensitive areas in the school curriculum. The most obvious of these will be the teaching of history. As noted in Chapter 6 there has been a tendency to adopt different versions of history, as of everything else, in Northern Ireland. This will be a key area where attempts to promote education for mutual understanding will undoubtedly face problems.

A second 'delicate' area involves rather more the 'hidden curriculum' of Northern Irish schools and therefore will perhaps be all the more difficult to embrace. This is the way in which schools in Northern Ireland approach the question of moral attitudes and values. The research reviewed in Chapter 4 has indicated that there is a suspicion that Northern Ireland is a society which adopts rather more rigid moral criteria than for example, English society. On the one hand this may well be a plus factor for Northern Ireland and in particular may have been a key element in enabling Northern Ireland to cope successfully with the potentially amoral influences arising from the conflict over the last fifteen years. On the other hand rigid moral standards also imply a general lack of tolerance. It is not surprising therefore that Breslin (1982) found that in Ireland, north and south, those young people who were operating at the highest levels of moral reasoning also showed most tolerance. Perhaps more importantly in the present context she also demonstrated that those children who had had an opportunity to engage in discussions involving controversial social and political issues were more likely to be operating at a more complex level of moral reasoning. As she points out the results of her study 'underscore the importance of recognising moral education as a precursor of tolerance and of incorporating a discussion of controversial issues into the school curriculum.'

Whether this will be accomplished in Northern Ireland's schools and whether society in Northern Ireland as a whole will indeed accept education for mutual understanding and tolerant relationships as 'the fourth "R" in the curriculum' (Government Press Release, 1985) remains to be seen. Certainly those who are attempting to promote this work must not underestimate the possibility that in some quarters their work may be seen as misinterpreting history and challenging basic moral standards. Nevertheless they will hopefully not be too easily discouraged because it would appear from both a theoretical and practical viewpoint that in the 'schools together' movement lies the best hope for the establishment of better community relations which in turn may one day bring peace to Northern Ireland.

Conclusions

Predicting the future is never an easy exercise and this is particularly true in a volatile political situation such as that in Northern Ireland. Nevertheless, an examination of the present generation of children and young people in Northern Ireland points to the obvious prediction that in the future little will change politically in this divided society. This prediction is reinforced by orthodox teaching in political socialisation which suggests that children learn or are taught, but certainly somehow acquire their basic political attitudes and behaviours from their parents. At present there is little evidence that young people in Northern Ireland are in any way rebelling against the ideas, political or otherwise of the older generation.

This goes against the rather more popular prediction which had tended to agree with the biblical assertion that 'the fathers having eaten sour grapes the children's teeth will be set on edge.' In other words, that the next generations of Northern Irish adults will not simply replicate the conflict of their fathers and mothers but will intensify it. It could, of course, be claimed that there is some evidence to support this idea, for example the claim that many young people in Northern Ireland are opting out of politics even to the extent of leaving Northern Ireland never to return. Also it has been pointed out that for the violence to escalate the paramilitary organisations do not need to recruit every young person in Northern Ireland. Instead, all that is required is that they produce a small number of dedicated revolutionaries in each generation.

Whatever the exact position this almost certainly means that the prediction that one day the conflict will simply fade away and peace will return is the least likely outcome of all for the future of Northern Ireland. However, it is still possible that peace may break out some day but only if positive steps are taken to ensure that the right climate of opinion is developed. For this to happen more attention will have to be paid by peacemakers to theoretical as well as practical issues. In particular it must be realised that interpersonal contact *per se* will not serve to end the conflict. This will only be achieved when through contact at the intergroup level new social categories and hence new social identities emerge.

Paradoxically there is also the question of making Northern Irish children more rebellious not less. Northern Ireland is undoubtedly a conservative, some would argue authoritarian society. Of course, in every society an attempt is made to transmit information, including attitudes and values from one generation to the next. In order to do this efficiently it has been suggested, the first step is that each child 'has to be moulded into an information acceptor. It has to be ready to believe what it is told.' (Waddington, 1960, 28). Unfortunately, adults in Northern Ireland, the evidence suggests, may have become all too expert at this process and therefore there is a need for children in Northern Ireland also to learn to question what they are told. Here there may also be an important if difficult role for the schools which ultimately could contribute to a Northern Ireland where two communities could live in peace rather that eternal conflict.

None of this can, of course, happen overnight. It will be a long slow process. But the fact that instant results are not achieved must not allow those who advocate peacemaking activities, particularly those in power, to lose faith with this approach because in the last analysis it could be argued this is Northern Ireland's only real hope.

References

Akenson, D. H., *Education and Enmity: The Control of Schooling in Northern Ireland 1920-50*, David & Charles, 1973.

Amir, Y., 'Contact Hypothesis in Ethnic Relations', *Psychological Bulletin*, 1969, 71, 319-42.

Austin, R., 'Playground culture in Northern Ireland', *Junior Education*, November, 1986.

Bandura, A. and Walters, R. H., *Social Learning and Personality Development*, New York, Holt, Rinehart and Winston, 1963.

Banks, W. C., 'White Preference in Blacks: A Paradigm in search of a Phenomenon', *Psychological Bulletin*, 1976, 83, 6, 1178-86.

Barner-Berry, C. and Rosenwein, R., *Psychological Perspectives on Politics*, Englewood Cliffs, N.J., Prentice-Hall, 1985.

Barritt, D. P. and Carter, C. F., *The Northern Ireland Problem: A Study in Group Relations*, Oxford University Press, 1962.

Beloff, H., 'A place not so far apart: conclusions of an outsider', in Harbison, J. and Harbison, J. (eds.), *A Society Under Stress: Children and Young People in Northern Ireland*, Somerset, Open Books, 1980.

Blease, M., 'Maladjusted School Children in a Belfast Centre', in Harbison, J. (ed.), *Children of the Troubles: Children in Northern Ireland*, Belfast, Stranmillis College Learning Resources Unit, 1983.

Blumler, J. C., 'Ulster on the Small Screen', *New Society*, 1971, 18, 1248-50.

Boal, F. W. and Orr, J. A. E., 'Ethnic and Temporal Dimensions of Regional Residential Preferences: A Northern Ireland Example', *Irish Geography*, 1978, 11, 35-53.

Bodman, F., 'War conditions and the mental health of the child', *British Medical Journal*, 1941, 2, 486-488.

Boyle, K. and Hadden, T., *Ireland: A Positive Proposal*, Penguin, 1985.

Boyle, K., Chesney, R. and Hadden, T., 'Who are the Terrorists?' *New*

Society, 1976, 6 May, 299.

Boyle, J., Jackson, J., Miller, B. and Roche, S., 'Attitudes in Ireland: Report No.1.', unpublished paper, Trinity College Dublin, 1976.

Breslin, A., 'Tolerance and moral reasoning among adolescents in Ireland', *Journal of Moral Education*, 1982, 11, 2, 112-27.

Brown, R. J. and Turner, J. C., 'Interpersonal and Intergroup Behaviour', in Turner, J. C. and Giles, H. (eds.), *Intergroup Behaviour*, Oxford, Basil Blackwell, 1981.

Burton, F., *The Politics of Legitimacy*, London, Routledge and Kegan Paul, 1979.

Cairns, E., 'The Development of Ethnic Discrimination in Young Children in Northern Ireland', in J. Harbison and J. Harbison (eds.), *Children and Young People in Northern Ireland: A Society Under Stress*, Somerset, Open Books, 1980.

Cairns, E., 'Children and the television news', unpublished paper, 1981.

Cairns, E., 'Northern Irish children's perceptions of the level of neighbourhood violence', unpublished paper, 1982a.

Cairns, E., 'Intergroup Conflict in Northern Ireland', in H. Tajfel (ed.), *Social Identity and Intergroup Relations*, Cambridge University Press, 1982b.

Cairns, E., 'Children's perceptions of normative and prescriptive interpersonal aggression in high and low areas of violence in Northern Ireland', unpublished paper 1983a.

Cairns, E., *The Role of Ethnic Identity in the Northern Irish Conflict*, paper presented to the sixth annual scientific meeting of the International Society of Political Psychology, Oxford, 1983b.

Cairns, E., 'The Political Socialisation of Tomorrow's Parents: Violence, Politics and the Media', in Harbison, J. (ed.), *Children of the Troubles: Children in Northern Ireland*, Belfast, Stranmillis College Learning Resources Unit, 1983c.

Cairns, E., 'Television news as a source of knowledge about the violence for children in Ireland: a test of the knowledge-gap hypothesis', *Current Psychological Research and Reviews*, 1984, Winter, 32-8.

Cairns, E. and Conlin, L., 'Children's moral reasoning and the Northern Irish violence', unpublished paper, 1985.

Cairns, E. and Duriez, B., 'The influence of speaker's accent on recall by Catholic and Protestant school children in Northern Ireland', *British Journal of Social and Clinical Psychology*, 1976, 15, 441-2.

Cairns, E., Hunter, D. and Herring, L., 'Young children's awareness of violence in Northern Ireland: The influence of Northern Irish television in Scotland and Northern Ireland', *British Journal of Social and Clinical Psychology*, 1980, 19, 3-6.

Cairns, E. and Mercer, G. W., 'Social Identity in Northern Ireland', *Human Relations*, 1984, 37, 12, 1095-1102.

Cairns, E. and Wilson, R., 'The impact of political violence on mild psychiatric morbidity in Northern Ireland', *British Journal of Psychiatry*, 1984, 145, 631-5.

Caul, B., 'Juvenile offenders in Northern Ireland – a statistical review', in Caul, B., Pinkerton, J. and Powell, F. (eds.), *The Juvenile Justice System in Northern Ireland*, Belfast, Ulster Polytechnic, 1983.

Commentary on Northern Ireland Crime Statistics, 1969-82, PPRU Occasional Paper 5, Belfast, Social Research Division, Policy, Planning and Research Unit, Department of Finance and Personnel, 1984.

Continuous Household Survey: Religion 6, PPRU Monitor No.2, June 1985.

Cox, H., 'The 1983 general Election in Northern Ireland: Anatomy and Consequences', *Parliamentary Affairs*, 1984, 37, 1, 40-58.

Curran, D., *Deviant attitudes and personality of juvenile scheduled and juvenile delinquent offenders*, paper presented at the annual conference of the British Psychological Society, Aberdeen, 1980.

Curran, D., 'Juvenile offending, civil disturbance and political terrorism – a psychological perspective', unpublished paper, 1984.

Darby, J., 'Divisiveness in Education', *The Northern Teacher*, 1973, Winter, 3-12.

Darby, J., 'History in the Schools', *Community Forum*, 1974, 4, 2.

Darby, J., *Conflict in Northern Ireland*, Dublin, Gill & Macmillan, 1976.

Darby, J. (ed.), *Northern Ireland: The Background to the Conflict*, Belfast, Appletree Press and New York, Syracuse University Press, 1983.

Darby, J. and Morris, G., 'Intimidation in Housing', *Community Forum*, 1973, 2, 7-11.

Darby, J., Murray, D., Batts, D., Dunn, S., Farren, S. and Harris, J., *Education and Community in Northern Ireland: Schools Apart?*, Coleraine, New University of Ulster, 1977.

Davies, J. and Turner, I.F., 'Friendship Choices in an Integrated Primary School in Northern Ireland', *The British Journal of Social Psychology*, 1984, 23, 2, 185-6.

Devlin, B., *The Price of My Soul*, Pan, 1969.

Dunn, S., Darby, J. and Mullan, K., *Schools Together?*, Coleraine, Centre for the Study of Conflict, University of Ulster, 1984.

Elliott, P., 'Misreporting Ulster: News as a field-dressing', *New Society*, 1976, 25 November, 398-401.

Elliot, R., and Lockhart, W.H., 'Characteristics of scheduled offenders and juvenile delinquents', in Harbison J. and Harbison J. (eds.), *A Society Under Stress: Children and Young People in Northern Ireland*, Somerset, Open Books, 1980.

Epstein, A. L., *Ethos and Identity*, London, Tavestock, 1978.

Erikson, E. H., *Identity, Youth and Crisis*, New York, Norton, 1968.

Evason, E., *Poverty: The Facts in Northern Ireland*, Poverty Pamphlet 27, Child Poverty Action Group, London, 1976.

Fee, F., 'Responses to a behavioural questionnaire of a group of Belfast children', in Harbison, J., and Harbison, J. (eds), *A Society Under Stress: Children and Young People in Northern Ireland*, Somerset, Open Books, 1980.

Fee, F., 'Education change in Belfast school children 1975-81', in Harbison, J. (ed.), *Children of the Troubles: Children in Northern Ireland*, Belfast, Stranmillis College Learning Resources Unit, 1983.

Fields, R. N., *A Society on the Run: A Psychology of Northern Ireland*, Middlesex, Penguin, 1973.

Fields, R. M., 'Psychological genocide: The children of Northern Ireland', *History of Childhood Quarterly: The Journal of Psychohistory*, 1975, 3, 201, 224.

Fraser, M., 'At School During Guerilla War', *Special Education*, 1972, 61, 6-8.

Fraser, M., *Children in Conflict*, Middlesex, Penguin, 1974.

Gamble, R., 'An Investigation in the Social Interaction, Identity and Religious Attitudes of Integrated Mill School Pupils', unpublished M.Sc. thesis, Queen's University, Belfast, 1982.

Gibbs, J., Arnold, K., Morgan, R., Schwartz, E., Cavanagh, M. and Tappan, M., 'Construction and Validation of a Multiple Choice Measure of Moral Reasoning', *Child Development*, 1984, 55, 527-36.

Giles, H. and Johnston, P., 'The Role of Language in Ethnic Group Relations', in Turner, J. C. and Giles, H. (eds.), *Intergroup Behaviour*, Oxford, Blackwell, 1983.

Greenstein, F. I., *Children and Politics*, (revised ed.), New Have Comm, Yale University Press, 1969.

Greer, J., 'The persistence of religion, a study of adolescents in Northern Ireland', *Character Potential*, 1980, 9, 139-49.

Greer, J., 'Viewing "the Other Side" in Northern Ireland: Openess and

Attitudes to Religion Among Catholic and Protestant Adolescents', *Journal for the Scientific Study of Religion*, 1985, 24, 3, 275-92.

Harbison, J., *Some possible effects of the two educational systems in Northern Ireland*, paper presented to the annual conference of the International Society for the Study of Political Psychology, Boston, 1980.

Harbison, J. J., 'Children in a Society in Turmoil', in Harbison, J. (ed.), *Children of the Troubles: Children in Northern Ireland*, Belfast, Stranmillis College Learning Resources Unit, 1983.

Heskin, K., 'Societal disintegration in Northern Ireland: Fact or fiction?', *The Economic and Social Review*, 1981, 12, 2, 97-113.

Heskin, K., 'Children and young people in Northern Ireland: A research review', in, Harbison, J. and Harbison, J. (eds.), *A Society Under Stress: Children and young people in Northern Ireland*, Somerset, Open Books, 1980a.

Heskin, K., *Northern Ireland: A Psychological Analysis*, Dublin, Gill & Macmillan, 1980b.

Hosin, A., *The impact of international conflict on children's and adolescents' national perceptions: A cross-cultural study in political socialisation*, D. Phil. thesis New University of Ulster, 1983.

Hosin, A. and Cairns, E., 'The impact of conflict on children's ideas about their country', *The Journal of Psychology*, 1984, 118(2), 161-68.

International Youth Bridge, Young Ideas in Northern Ireland: Christian Belief and Life Style among Young Adults in Northern Ireland, Belfast, City of Belfast YMCA, 1985.

Jackson, H., *The Two Irelands – A Dual Study of Intergroup Tensions*, London, Minority Rights Group Report No. 2, 1971.

Jahoda, G. and Harrison, S., 'Belfast Children: Some effects of a Conflict Environment', *Irish Journal of Psychology*, 1975, 3, 1, 1-19.

Jardine, E., 'Police cautioning in Northern Ireland', *Lynx*, 1983.

Jenkins, R. and McCrae, J., *Religion, Conflict and Polarization in Northern Ireland*, Lancaster, Peace Research Centre, 1966.

Kahn, J. V., 'Moral Reasoning in Irish Children and Adolescents as measured by the Defining Issues Test', *Irish Journal of Psychology*, 1982, 2, 96-108.

Kelly, G. A., *The Psychology of Personal Constructs*, New York, Norton, 1955.

Knutson, J. N., 'Victimization as a Root of Political Violence', unpublished paper, University of California, Los Angeles, 1981.

Kuhn, M. H. and Mcpartland, S., 'An empirical investigation of self-attitudes', *American Sociological Review*, 1954, 19, 68-76.

Lawless, H., 'Understanding of and identity with national and religious groups in young Northern Ireland children: The influence of conflict and contact', unpublished B.Sc. thesis, Queen's University Belfast, 1981.

Lockhart, W. H. and Elliott, R., 'Changes in the Attitudes of Young Offenders in an Integrated Assessment Centre', in Harbison, J. and Harbison, J. (eds.), *A Society Under Stress: Children and Young People in Northern Ireland*, Somerset, Open Books, 1980.

Lyle, J. and Hoffman, H. R., 'Children's Use of Television and Other Media', in E. A. Rubinstein, G. A. Comstock and J. P. Murray (eds.), *Television and Social Behaviour*, Vol.4, *Television in Day-to-Day Life: Patterns of use*, Washington, Gov. Print Off., 1972.

Lyons, H. A., 'Psychiatric Sequalae of the Belfast Riots', *British Journal of Psychiatry*, 1971, 118(544), 265-73.

Lyons, H. A., 'Riots and rioters in Belfast – Demographic analysis of 1,674 arrestees in a two year period', *Economic and Social Review*, 1972, 3(4), 605-14a.

Lyons, H. A., 'Depressive illness and aggression in Belfast', *British Medical Journal*, 1972, 1(5796), 342-344b.

Lyons, H. A., 'The psychological effects of the civil disturbances on children', *The Northern Teacher*, 1973, Winter, 35-38.

Malone, J., 'Schools and Community Relations', *The Northern Teacher*, 1973, Winter, 19-30.

McAulay, M. and Cunningham, G., 'Intermediate treatment and residential provisions for juvenile offenders in Northern Ireland – A Whitfield House perspective', in Caul, B., Pinkerton, J. and Powell, F. (eds.), *The Juvenile Justice System in Northern Ireland*, Belfast, Ulster Polytechnic, 1983.

McAuley, R. and Troy, M., 'The impact of urban conflict and violence on children referred to a child guidance clinic', in Harbison, J. (ed.), *Children of The Troubles: Children in Northern Ireland*, Belfast, Stranmillis College Learning Resources Unit, 1983.

McCann, E., *War in An Irish Town*, Middlesex, Penguin, 1974.

McCartney, C., *An Overview of Reconciliation Projects*, paper presented to the conference Contact and the Reconciliation of Conflict, Belfast, 1985.

McFarlane, W. G., 'Mixed Marriages in Ballycuan, Northern Ireland', *Journal of Comparative Family Studies*, 1979, 10, 191-205.

McGrath, A., and Wilson, R., *Factors which influence the prevalence and variation of psychological problems in children in Northern Ireland*, paper read to the Annual Conference of the Development Section of the British Psychological Society, Belfast, 1985.

McIvor, M., *Northern Ireland: A preliminary look at environmental awareness*, paper presented at the Sixth Biennial Conference of the International Society of the Study of Behavioural Development, Toronto, 1981.

McKeown, M., 'Civil Unrest: Secondary School's Survey', *The Northern Teacher*, 1973, Winter, 39-42.

McKernan, J., 'Pupil values as social indicators of intergroup differences in Northern Ireland', in Harbison, J. and Harbison, J. (eds.), *A Society Under Stress: Children and Young People in Northern Ireland*, Somerset, Open Books, 1980.

McWhirter, L., *The Influence of Contact on the Development of Interpersonal Awareness in Northern Ireland Children*, paper read to the Annual Conference of the Development Section of the British Psychological Society, Manchester, 1981.

McWhirter, L., 'Northern Irish Children's Conceptions of Violent Crime', *The Howard Journal*, 1982, 21, 167-77.

McWhirter, L., *How 'troubled' are children in Northern Ireland compared to children living outside Northern Ireland?*, paper presented to the Annual Conference of the Psychological Society of Ireland, Athlone, 1983a.

McWhirter, L., 'Looking Back and Looking Forward: An Inside Perspective', in Harbison, J. (ed.), *Children of the Troubles: Children in Northern Ireland*, Belfast, Stranmillis College Learning Resources Unit, 1983b.

McWhirter, L., 'Contact and Conflict: The Question of Integrated Education', *The Irish Journal of Psychology*, 1983, vi, 13-27c.

McWhirter, L., *Northern Ireland: Visions of the Future*, paper presented at the Annual Conference of the Northern Ireland Branch of the British Psychological Society, Rosapenna, Co. Donegal, 1983d.

McWhirter, L., *Is getting caught in a riot more stressful for children than seeing a scary film or moving to a new school?*, paper presented to the Annual Conference of the Northern Ireland Branch of the Psychological Society, Portballintrae, 1984.

McWhirter, L. and Gamble, R., 'Development of ethnic awareness in the absence of physical cues', *The Irish Journal of Psychology*, 1982, 5, 109-27.

McWhirter, L. and Trew, K., 'Social Awareness in Northern Ireland children: Myth and Reality', *Bulletin of the British Psychological Society*, 1981, 34, 308-11.

McWhirter, L. and Trew, K., *Contact and Conflict: Evaluating Reconciliation Projects*, paper presented to the Annual Conference of the British Psychological Society, Swansea, 1985.

McWhirter, L., Young, V. and Majury, J., 'Belfast children's awareness of violent death', *British Journal of Social Psychology*, 1983, 22, 2, 81-92.

Mercer, G. W. and Bunting, B., 'Some motivations of adolescent demonstrators in the Northern Ireland civil disturbances', in Harbison, J. and Harbison, J. (eds.), *A Society Under Stress: Children and Young People in Northern Ireland*, Somerset, Open Books, 1980.

Milner, D., *Children and Race*, Middlesex, Penguin, 1975.

Mitchell, J. K., 'Social violence in Northern Ireland', *Geographical Review*, 1979, 69, 2, 179-201.

Moxon-Browne, E., *Nation, Class and Creed in Northern Ireland*, Aldershot, Gower, 1983.

Mullan, E., 'Theoretical investigation of the salience of religion and national identity in Northern Ireland', unpublished B.A. thesis, Queen's University, Belfast, 1982.

Murray, D., 'Schools and conflict', in Darby, J. (ed.), *Northern Ireland: The Background to the Conflict*, Belfast, Appletree Press, 1983.

Murray, R., 'Political Violence in Northern Ireland 1969-1977', in Boal, F. W. and Douglas, J. N. H. (eds.), *Integration and Division: Geographical Perspectives on the Northern Ireland problem*, London, Academic Press, 1982.

Murray, R. C. and Boal, F. W., 'Forced residential mobility in Belfast 1969-72', in Harbison, J. and Harbison, J. (eds.), *A Society Under Stress: Children and Young People in Northern Ireland*, Somerset, Open Books, 1980.

Nobles, W. W., 'Psychological research and the Black self-concept: A critical review', *Journal of Social Issues*, 1973, 29, 1, 11-31.

O'Donnell, E. E., *Northern Irish Stereotypes*, Dublin, College of Industrial Relations, 1977.

Osborne, R. D., Cormack, R. J., Reid, N. G. and Williamson, A. P., 'Political Arithmetic, Higher Education and Religion in Northern Ireland', in Cormack, R. J. and Osborne, R. D. (eds.), *Religion, Education and Employment: Aspects of equal opportunity in Northern Ireland*, Belfast, Appletree Press, 1983.

Owens, D. J. and Straus, M. A., 'The social structure of violence in childhood and approval of violence as an adult', *Aggressive Behaviour*, 1975, 1, (3), 193-211.

de Paor, L., *Divided Ulster*, Middlesex, Penguin, 1970.

Persistent School Absenteeism in Northern Ireland, Belfast, Department of Education for Northern Ireland, 1977 and 1982.

Poole, M., 'Religious Segregation in Urban Northern Ireland', in Boal, F. W. and Douglas, J. N. H. (eds.), *Integration and Division: Geographical Perspectives on the Northern Ireland Problem*, London, Academic Press, 1982.

Poole, M., 'The Demography of Violence', in Darby, J. (ed.), *Northern Ireland: The Background to the Conflict*, Belfast, Appletree Press, 1983.

du Preez, P. D., Bhana, K., Broekman, N., Lauw, J. and Nel, E., 'Ideology and Utopia Revisited', *Social Dynamics*, 1981, 7(1), 52-55.

Report of the National Advisory Commission on Civil Disorders, New York, Bantam Books, 1968.

Robinson, A., 'Education and Sectarian Conflict in Northern Ireland', *New Era*, 1971, 52, 384-8.

Rose, R., *Governing Without Consensus: An Irish Perspective*, London, Faber & Faber, 1971.

Rose, R., *Northern Ireland: A Time of Choice*, New York, Macmillan, 1976.

Ross, R., 'The reliability of the Twenty Statements test', unpublished B.Sc. thesis, New University of Ulster, 1981.

Russell, J., 'Socialisation and Conflict', unpublished Ph.D. thesis, University of Strathclyde, 1974.

Rutter, M., 'A child's behavioural questionnaire for completion by teachers: preliminary findings', *Journal of Child Psychology and Psychiatry*, 1967, 8, 1-11.

Rutter, M., 'Stress, Coping, and Development: Some issues and some questions', in Garhezy, N. and Rutter, M. (eds.), *Stress coping and development in children*, New York, McGraw Hill, 1983.

Rutter, M., Cox, A., Tupling, C., Berger, M. and Yule, W., 'Attainment and adjustment in two geographical areas: I. the prevalence of psychiatric disorder', *British Journal of Psychiatry*, 1975, 126, 520-33.

Schellenberg, J. A., 'Area variations of violence in Northern Ireland', *Sociological Focus*, 1977, 10, 69-79.

Seeman, M. V., 'The Psychopathology of Everyday Names', *British*

Journal of Medical Psychology, 1976, 49, 89-95.

Stewart, A. T. Q., *The Narrow Ground: Aspects of Ulster*, London, Faber & Faber, 1977.

Simpson, J., 'Economic Development. Cause or effect in the Northern Ireland Conflict', in Darby, J. (ed.), *Northern Ireland: The Background to the Conflict*, Belfast, Appletree Press, 1983.

Stringer, M., 'The Utility of Stereotypic Face Stimuli as Disguised Measures of Intergroup Attitudes in Northern Ireland', unpublished D.Phil. Thesis, New University of Ulster, 1984.

Stringer, M. and Cairns, E., 'Catholic and Protestant Young People's Rating of Stereotyped Protestant and Catholic Faces', *British Journal of Social Psychology*, 1983, 22, 241-46.

Taggart, G., 'Social awareness and social reasoning in a sample of Northern Ireland children and adolescents', unpublished B.A. thesis, Queen's University, Belfast, 1980.

Tapp, J. L. and Kohlberg, L., 'Developing sense of law and legal justice', *The Journal of Social Issues*, 1971, 27, 65-91.

Taylor, L. and Nelson, S. (eds.), *Young people and civil conflict in Northern Ireland*, Belfast, D.H.S.S., 1977.

Tajfel, H., *Differentiation between social groups: Studies in the social psychology of intergroup relations*, London, Academic Press, 1978.

Terchek, R. J., 'Options to Stress: Emigration and Militancy in Northern Ireland', *Social Indicators Research*, 1984, 15, 4, 351-87.

Thomas, M. H. and Drabman, R. S., *Effects of Television Violence on Expectations of Others' Aggression*, paper presented to the Annual Conference of the American Psychological Association, 1977.

Thompson, J. L. P., 'Denial, Polarization and Genocidal Massacre: A Comparative Analysis of Northern Ireland and Zanzibar', *The Economic and Social Review*, 1986, 17, 4, 293-314.

Trew, K., *Social Identity and Group Membership*, paper presented to the Annual Conference of the British Psychological Society, Northern Irish Branch, Rosapenna, 1981a.

Trew, K., *Intergroup relations and the development of social identity in Northern Ireland*, paper presented at the 6th Biennial Conference of the International Society for the Study of Behavioural Development, Ontario, Canada, 1981b.

Trew, K., 'Group Identification in a Divided Society', in Harbison, J. (ed.), *Children of the Troubles: Children in Northern Ireland*, Belfast, Stranmillis College Learning Resources Unit, 1983.

Trew, K. and McWhirter, L., 'Conflict in Northern Ireland: A Research

Perspective', in Stringer, P. (ed.), *Confronting Social Issues Vol. 2. European Monographs in Social Psychology*, London, Academic Press, 1982.

Turner, E. B., Turner, I. F. and Reid, A., 'Religious attitudes in two types of urban secondary schools: a decade of change', *The Irish Journal of Education*, 1980, 14, 1, 43-52.

Ungoed-Thomas, J. R , 'Patterns of Adolescent Behaviour and Relationships in Northern Ireland', *Journal of Moral Education*, 1972, 2, 53-61.

Utley, T. E., *Lessons of Ulster*, London, J. M. Dent and Sons Ltd., 1975.

Violence in Ireland: A Report to the Churches, Belfast, Christian Journals Ltd., 1976.

Waddington, C. H., *The Ethical Animal*, Chicago, Illinois, University of Chicago Press, 1960.

Weinreich, P., *A Manual for Identity Exploration Using Personal Constructs*, London, SSRC, 1980.

Weinreich, P., 'Identity development in Protestant and Roman Catholic adolescent boys and girls in Belfast', paper presented to the 10th International Congress of the International Association for Child and Adolescent Psychiatry and Allied Professions, Dublin, 1982.

Williamson, A., Reid, N., Cormack, R. and Osborne, R., 'The characteristics of Ulster's students', *Times Higher Education Supplement*, 1982, 8, 10-11.

Wright, D. and Cox, E., 'Changes in moral belief among sixth-form boys and girls over a seven-year period in relation to religious belief, age and sex differences', *The British Journal of Social and Clinical Psychology*, 1971, 10, 4, 332-41.

Whyte, Jean, 'Control and supervision of urban 12-year-olds within and outside Northern Ireland: a pilot study', *Irish Journal of Psychology*, 1983, 6, 37-45a.

Whyte, Jean, 'Everyday life for 11 and 12-year-olds in a troubled area of Belfast: do "the troubles" intrude?', in Harbison, J. (ed.), *Children of the Troubles: Children in Northern Ireland*, Belfast, Stranmillis College Learning Resources Unit, 1983b.

Ziv, A., Kruglanski, A. W. and Schulman, S., 'Children's psychological reactions to wartime stress', *Journal of Personality and Social Psychology*, 1974, 30, 24-30.

Index